THE LIEDER OF RICHARD STRAUSS

The Lieder of Richard Strauss

ALAN JEFFERSON

PRAEGER PUBLISHERS
New York · Washington

BOOKS THAT MATTER

Published in the United States of America in 1971
by Praeger Publishers, Inc., 111 Fourth Avenue,
New York, N.Y. 10003

Library of Congress Catalog Card Number: 77-141650

Printed in Great Britain

For Kate

Contents

Introduction

Richard Strauss wrote 205 lieder—that is to say, songs—either for voice and piano or for voice and orchestra. (I shall later be explaining this apparent contradiction—the original meaning of the word *Lied* did not include or anticipate an orchestral accompaniment.) Thirty-four of these songs, written before the first group published by Strauss with an opus number, have always been considered immature, and—together with another six which occur chronologically between the first acknowledged group of songs (opus 10) and the second (opus 15)—are known as the *Jugendlieder*.

I might have treated each of the songs in Strauss's output in equal depth and detail, yet had I done so the result would have been little more than notes on each; while to move through the songs in strict chronological order, leaving many of them out, would have robbed the process of its purpose. What I looked for then was a new sort of grouping. Because the songs are never sung as sets, as they were composed and published—with a few notable exceptions which will be apparent—I arrived at the principle of classification by subject, irrespective of date of composition or opus number. Since these subject-groups include the most frequently performed and many of the most beautiful and also most significant of Strauss's lieder, I shall almost certainly have included most of those familiar to the reader. Now that very nearly all the songs have been recorded and—apart from the *Jugendlieder*—are available to be heard, some which until recently were entirely unknown may well be taken up by singers at recitals, and several of these have been included here. I have also dealt with three other songs which by their constitution are unusual.

I have said a good deal about the orchestrated and the orchestral songs because these form a central point of my argument; but I have said little or nothing about actual interpretation. The mechanics are sometimes there, but the magic cannot be. I am neither lieder-singer nor accompanist by profession, and I know that this specialized group of artists includes many who are far better equipped to write about their art than I am. It is they alone who should deal with interpretation, which, after all, is a very personal skill, acquired only after much experience. For example, one aspect peculiar to the lied is that the accompanist must be able to transpose up or down on demand to suit the singer: thus the key is not sacred, as it is in all other kinds of composition (except possibly the occasional operatic aria).

I have described the circumstances surrounding most of the lieder I have discussed, and a full list of them in Appendix C will indicate how they fall within Strauss's main output as well as in relationship to one another.

Since Richard Strauss composed all the songs under discussion, often accompanied them himself and preferred his wife to sing many of them above all other interpreters, his personality and relationship with his wife and those round him are important to a fuller understanding of the man and his songs. The biographical chapter about Strauss as composer, conductor and musician extraordinary, first under the Kaiser and then in Hitler's Germany, is intended both to supply this need and to clarify a picture which has often been blurred by his detractors on grounds of jealousy, race, politics or sheer misunderstanding.

I have also devoted considerable space to Strauss's harmonic progressions during the songs, hoping that this will be of help to readers who wish to try them out on the piano or to look at them from the technical angle. For, after all, this book is intended not only as a reference book to the lieder, but also as an introduction to them for the newcomer to this branch of music, even to this part of Strauss's art.

Finally, I am grateful to Messrs Boosey and Hawkes for permission to reproduce music from their collected edition of Strauss's songs.

Guildford
June 1971

ALAN JEFFERSON

1 Richard Strauss at the Centre of his Time

Richard Strauss lived from 1864 to 1949: from the American Civil War almost until the Korean War. His life was disrupted and many of his plans shattered by the two world wars of 1914–18 and 1939–45. If this seems to attach too much importance to military history in a book about a musician and his work, it is only because it is wars that change a man's way of life more radically than anything else, and it was change that Strauss attempted to avoid all through his life.

He was born on 11 June 1864, the son of Germany's most famous horn-player, Franz Strauss, and his wife Josephine, a daughter of the Munich brewing family of Pschorr. It was the age of Bismarck, and of the emergence of Prussia as a formidable world power. These were stirring days for Germany, and every young German was brought up to believe in his Fatherland and to hold his head high—as indeed British boys were taught to do in Queen Victoria's Great Britain.

Franz Strauss, as well as being an exceptional horn-player, was the conductor of the semi-professional Munich orchestra the Wilde Gung'l, a viola player in a Munich quartet, a composer of pieces for the horn, and a professor at the Academy. Consequently he was better qualified—and connected—than most parents to direct his son's musical education. Richard was brought up in comfort: there was no shortage of money, for although his parents were not exactly rich, they were comfortably provided for and made certain that their only son was encouraged in the fostering of his musical talent.

This was apparent at an early age. At Christmas 1870, when he was six and a half, Richard Strauss wrote his first composition. The 'Weihnachtslied' is said to have been notated by him, but had the words—of a poem by Schubart—written in by his mother. One might ask, why a song? Why not, say, a composition for his father's instrument, the horn, which was practised in the house at all hours? Perhaps because the young Strauss was able to sing this song himself, and by sheer experience (if we can call it that) felt what would 'go', by self-expression and experiment. This first composition was dedicated to his Uncle and Aunt Pschorr, his mother's brother George and his wife.*

When Strauss died at Garmisch-Partenkirchen on 8 September 1949, four songs had been his last completed compositions; a fifth lay unfinished on his desk. Thus lieder encompassed his working life: lieder which formed a substantial part of his output, and lieder such as no other composer had written, for Strauss's preoccupation with the human voice in his operas had given him a rare insight into its capabilities—particularly in the female register. Strauss's chief form of composition was of course opera, which provided him with far greater royalties than his other works, and it might be thought that fifteen—of which *Der Rosenkavalier* is almost certainly the all-time 'best-seller' among German operas—might have given Strauss his fill of composing for voices; but the opposite was the case and he never lost the desire nor the opportunity to glorify the human voice in aria and ensemble.

Not that Strauss was always writing songs, any more than he was always writing operas; yet providing he had the kind of words which appealed to him, which seized his imagination, he never had any difficulty in setting them, whether poem or libretto. Unfortunately, when no suitable words were offered, he was either forced to turn his attention elsewhere, or, worse still, made do with inferior material.

Strauss received his style, upon which he set his own particular signature, from both Wagner and Brahms, those two opposites from each of whom he took what he felt he most needed. His early choral work *Des Wandrers Sturmlied*, opus 14, is good writing for voices, in a particularly Brahmsian way. Yet he never proceeded further along the strictly Brahmsian path in vocal writing, and no songs which he wrote either before or after opus 14 show any special indebtedness to this composer. His lifelong admiration for Mozart, on the other hand, bordered on idolatry; he liked sometimes to think of certain works as tributes to Mozart, though never as challenges: he never presumed to outdo Mozart, for he knew he never could.

In fact Richard Strauss, for all his aloofness, hauteur and

* See p. 22.

wealth, knew himself only too well. Who but a man completely aware of his own limitations could have brought himself to say, when in his eighties, 'I am a first-class second-rate composer'? There is more than a grain of truth wrapped up in wry humour here. At times Strauss's music is remarkably uneven. While one can trace the inventive genius of Beethoven or of Wagner in a fairly systematic progression, Strauss's rises and falls like a British weather-chart: sometimes hitting peaks of glorious sunshine, only to fall back into dullness. Perhaps the 'brighter' compositions seem to shine more by comparison, but what is missing in the others is not skill—never skill, nor careful and applied thought—it is sheer inspiration. Strauss always had to be moved to create his best works, otherwise the mechanical composing faculty, beyond which his genius frequently deserted him, was all that there was. This faculty was a marvellous gift: it gave him the power to invent splendid vocal lines, rich harmonies, true symphonic progression within an opera act. But it was as iron to the pure gold of the great compositions. They were written with ease and as much skill, but the sparkle of more than a mere talent was there too. They came from the heart, not merely from the cool head. I have included, later on, one of these 'other' songs—'In goldener Fülle'.*

When Strauss was growing up and learning his craft in Munich the great composers of the day were Wagner and Brahms. He knew Brahms, but never met Wagner. Franz Strauss had worked for many years as Wagner's first horn, and had detested the composer as a man but played his works because it was his job. He had tried to keep his son away from the 'devilish music' but had failed, and had eventually given up, grudgingly. Strauss's first introduction to the score of *Tristan* had been a revelation, and thereafter he had read and played on the piano all the other operas. *Tristan* became for him the greatest test in opera conducting, the work in which more than in any other he tried to achieve a complete performance. This was at variance with his behaviour when he conducted some of his own operas: their very popularity and regularity of performance ensured Strauss's huge income, but he himself was utterly bored with the thought of them, and as time went on this began to show.

* See p. 85.

Strauss's first big success in composition was the symphonic poem *Don Juan*, based (wordlessly) on a poem by Lenau that dwells on the futility of the Don's amorous pursuits. Strauss conducted the first performance in Weimar on 11 November 1889 and was instantly recognized as a composer of integrity, importance and originality. Although Franz Liszt is usually credited with developing the form of the tone-poem, it was Strauss who deployed all the possibilities in it and brought it, more or less, to its fruition with the Sinfonia Domestica in 1903 —for this, although called a symphony, tells a family story almost bar by bar. The Alpine Symphony of 1915 is even more of a tone-poem than the Domestica, but the enormous and totally impractical orchestral forces (for wartime) may be said to have ruptured this form so far as Strauss was concerned. The Alpine Symphony is rarely performed today on grounds of expense.

Concurrently with the composition of other tone-poems—*Tod und Verklärung*, *Till Eulenspiegel*, *Also sprach Zarathustra*, *Don Quixote*, *Ein Heldenleben*—and up to the Domestica, Strauss was finding poems which inspired him to create melodies and turn them into lieder. Also, in the years 1887–93, not without extreme difficulty, he wrote a Wagner-type opera, *Guntram*, which was not a success when it appeared at Weimar in 1894. The leading soprano, Pauline de Ahna, the daughter of a general, became his wife in that same year. Clearly Strauss had had Pauline's voice in mind when writing *Guntram*, and his wedding-present to her was the set of lieder opus 27. They toured together giving lieder recitals from the time they were married and up to about 1915, so that Pauline's voice must have become closely identified in his mind with a great number of the songs. Perhaps this is one reason why Strauss became so bored, in later life, when the great favourites like 'Cäcilie', 'Morgen!' and 'Traum durch die Dämmerung' were sung in his presence by other artists.

From the time of his marriage, Strauss's home life was changed to one of inexorable routine. Frau Strauss may still be in many ways an enigma, but there was one very definite thing about her: she recognized her husband's weaknesses. These were a great fondness for the card-game *Skat* and a tendency to sloth so far as his work went. The days became rigorously divided into working-time, eating-time, walking-time and a little time for recreation. Strauss was conducting a great deal, too, and he was known all over Europe from Paris to Moscow as an interesting, *avant-garde* musician whose well-planned programmes contained new and old works so arranged as not to seem to thrust at audiences what Strauss thought was good for them. When he was abroad on conducting tours he kept in close touch with his wife, parents and friends by letter, while the excellent German railways got him about the country at a rate that most of our conductors today would declare to be impossible, even by air.

After *Guntram* Strauss produced, with the aid of a humorous writer called von Wolzogen, his second opera, *Feuersnot.* This was aimed not only at the philistines and hidebound bureaucrats everywhere, but specifically at the inhabitants of Munich, who had first turned out Wagner, had then retired Franz Strauss with the minimum of appreciation, and had finally made life impossible for Richard Strauss himself when he was on the staff of the Opera there. The opera was a moderate success for a while, though it is surprising that with its risqué plot and erotic score it was banned only at the Berlin Court Theatre.

Then in 1903, as he was putting the finishing touches to the Sinfonia Domestica, Strauss went to see a German version of Oscar Wilde's *Salome* in Berlin. The play made an instant impression upon him: his opera *Salome* was performed at the Dresden Court Opera on 9 December 1905 and was a sensational success. Strauss had managed somehow to distil all the decay and rottenness, all the perversion and sexuality of the main characters into his score (though he failed to make anything of John the Baptist). It was the beginning not only of a new style of composition but of a new direction in musical thought, and Strauss was at once recognized as the most advanced and interesting composer in Germany. His tone-poems had been adventurous, but nothing had been so hair-raisingly outrageous as *Salome.*

There were two major results. First, Strauss made so much from the opera that he was able to build an ideal house for himself at Garmisch. This looked onto the most glorious Alpine scenery, and, though it was sufficiently near to Munich and to the Italian border to make travelling an easy matter, was also reasonably remote, so that he was able to work without the interruptions that were to be expected in town and city. The building and occupation of this house were the first important product of the success of *Salome*. The other was that Hugo von Hofmannsthal, one of Austria's leading literary figures and perhaps her most significant poet, offered Strauss his adaptation of the *Electra* of Sophocles as a libretto. Strauss agreed—having previously ignored requests from Hofmannsthal to collaborate on operas—and the result was the most important opera, musically, that he wrote. *Elektra* pursued the treatment which Strauss had used in *Salome* and pushed it to the farthest edges of tonality, using marvellous orchestral colours, mixing savage moods with contemplative and breathtakingly beautiful ones, all to highlight and uplift Greek tragedy beyond anything anybody had done before.

Elektra was first performed at Dresden on 25 January 1909, and brought Strauss to the crossroads of his life. Had he gone straight on in the direction in which *Salome* and *Elektra* both pointed, one can only conjecture at the result. Perhaps he could not have gone on—perhaps *Elektra* was the furthest that his thought could reach. He did ask and go on asking Hofmannsthal to provide him with libretti for other wild and terrible operas, but Hofmannsthal scoffed at the idea. He had, he considered, far better thoughts, far purer and more poetical than any of that sort of nonsense. What Strauss got from Hofmannsthal was *Der Rosenkavalier*.

To move from *Elektra* to *Der Rosenkavalier* might seem to need a visit to Italy, or at least to Vienna; some careful thought to clear the mind and prepare it for a return to the lusciousness of the Domestica and *Feuersnot*. But to Strauss there was never any thought of 'going back'. He continued to compose, and accepted commissions to write for the Kaiser, turning out four military marches, a soldiers' song for male chorus and a brass work for an order of chivalry.

These were not from the heart. They were what his wife was then and thereafter to call 'note-spinning'—the automatic process at work. Small wonder under these circumstances, nevertheless, when Strauss must have found himself at a crossroads with *Der Rosenkavalier* pointing in the wrong direction.

The way was inviting enough, but it was still not the way in which he wanted to go. When this opera brought him a fortune he tried to repeat the process, to write another success and in the same vein. But he never did. And consequently he lost his position as the leading and most advanced composer in Germany, the pioneer of a 'new music'.

Every generation has its 'new music'. In the case of the up-and-coming generation in Europe, it was the Viennese School of Schoenberg, Berg and Webern. In the first years of the twentieth century they had been completely eclipsed by Strauss, but when Strauss faltered they were there to take his place, and they changed the direction of advanced musical thought towards what we now understand—or fail to understand—in Boulez, Messiaen, Nono and the other roots and branches of this newest of new music.

This did not mean that what Strauss had written was no longer played. It was: he became the richest composer—some say the richest man—in a Germany that included Krupp von Bohlen. He went on composing: *Ariadne auf Naxos*, *Josephslegende* (for the Diaghilev Ballet), the Alpine Symphony and *Die Frau ohne Schatten.* The stage-works were all to books by Hofmannsthal, and it is interesting to note in passing that Strauss never set any of his poems, except once in 1914, the Cantata for unaccompanied male voices. Strauss's own great knowledge of the classics and of poets past and present provided him with his song-poems; moreover, Hofmannsthal was not musical, and it is doubtful whether he was able to reduce his complex thoughts and simplify them for this medium, as a direct supplier of poems for setting. It seems that he never tried; certainly Strauss never asked him to do so.

The First World War, which broke out immediately after the failure of *Josephslegende*, brought with it for Strauss the sequestration of a fortune that he had invested in London. The effect of this was that he was still obliged, at the age of fifty, to continue conducting so as to keep his income up to the desired level, whereas he had planned to devote far less time to this arduous occupation and far more to sitting at home in Garmisch and composing. The shattering of his plans by politicians and warmongers angered Strauss. He felt that everything that was going on in the world was intended to upset him personally, and thus he failed to emerge as a tower of musical strength in the writing of patriotic marches and tunes. War was not for him. All he wanted was peace, and to be left alone without restrictions.

The restrictions upon luxuries greatly reduced the number of performances of his operas and orchestral compositions at home and abroad, and his income was seriously affected. The war dragged on, and so did the opera on which he and Hofmannsthal had been engaged when it started, *Die Frau ohne Schatten.*

The end of the war, in 1918, saw Strauss as temporary director of the Berlin State Opera and then as co-director with Franz Schalk of the Vienna State Opera. He had, moreover, spent a good deal of time and effort in helping to found two most valuable institutions: a Society of German Composers, designed to protect their interests; and the Salzburg Festival, which started in 1920, but plans for which had been under way since before 1917, when Strauss became one of the founders of the Festival Association.

In 1923, after five years' intermittent work, Strauss finished the composition of an opera for which he had written the libretto himself. This was *Intermezzo*, a continuation of the theme in the Domestica—himself, his wife and son. It was written in an entirely new style—for Strauss—a kind of *parlando*, with the rise and fall of natural speech faithfully reflected in the music. This naturalness in plot and treatment was anathema to Hofmannsthal, despite his politeness; and it cannot help but bring to mind the thought that no sooner had Strauss, however temporarily, disengaged himself from Hofmannsthal, than he produced a novel composition. This style was never reflected in Strauss's lieder—could scarcely be, considering the kind of poems which he chose to set.

Sadly, Strauss returned to Hofmannsthal for two more operas; and the novelty which *Intermezzo* might have engendered in the opera world had it been less parochial and *echt deutsch* was totally eclipsed by Alban Berg's *Wozzeck*, which emerged in 1925. This was not merely *parlando* but *Sprechgesang* and the twelve-tone scale together: considerably more advanced. *Intermezzo* at once became *ancien jeu*, and is regrettably neglected. It is a very charming work, full of lovely ideas, though in the context of 1924–5, they are already fading.

In the following year Strauss and Hofmannsthal made an attempt to take advantage of the new cinema craze by transferring the *Rosenkavalier* idea on to celluloid. The film appealed to a small audience, and when Strauss himself was commanding a pit orchestra and conducting his own arrangement of the augmented score to supply incidental music it might have been very interesting. But this obviously he could not do all the time. What did emerge was a set of gramophone records which he made in London of orchestral 'scenes' from the film, and this gives us an idea of how he played the score. That he never made a recording of the complete opera is a loss to posterity.

After a less than successful opera called *Die ägyptische Helena,* which, by Hofmannsthal's standards had an exceedingly weak second-act plot (the story virtually ends half-way through), they embarked upon what was to be their last collaboration, *Arabella.* A new Hofmannsthal–Strauss opera set in Vienna raised expectations of another *Rosenkavalier*—these hopes proving groundless, the work had only a limited showing and did not reach its peak of understanding and enjoyment until some fifteen years later. Hofmannsthal died before it was produced.

At seventy years of age Strauss was no longer adventurous, musically, in fact no longer courageous in any way, and therefore unable to deal with the immediate political situation.

He has been unfairly criticized for not having left Germany, or given Hitler an ultimatum, or taken an active part in trying to overthrow the new régime. None of these propositions is either sensible or practical. Furthermore, Strauss was in an awkward position: his son Franz had married a Jewess in 1924, and there were two sons of the union. In making Strauss head of the Reichsmusikkammer Hitler sought to relate him to the Nazis and to keep him as an ally; even if his racial record was smirched by his Jewish daughter-in-law, Strauss was still of great propaganda value.

Strauss was irreproachable artistically, but exceedingly naïve politically. Having accepted the honour from Hitler (he was not given the chance of refusing it) he twice found himself in a position where he seemed to be doing the right thing both as official and as artist by offering to conduct in moments of crisis. The first was at a Berlin Philharmonic concert, where the contents of the hall had been theatened with destruction if Bruno Walter—a Jew—fulfilled his contract as guest conductor. Strauss took over the concert to save it, and gave his fee to the musicians. Secondly, Toscanini refused to conduct *Parsifal* at Bayreuth, and also went out of his way to offend Hitler personally. Strauss once more stepped into the breach and saved *Parsifal*. It seems perfectly honest behaviour when looked at—as Strauss looked at it—musically; but both these events were used as propaganda against him. He never understood why.

At this time Strauss was working with Stefan Zweig on the opera *Die schweigsame Frau*. Zweig was being watched by the Gestapo, and when Strauss wrote him a letter in which he railed against all philistines, Germans included, it was intercepted and sent to Hitler. Strauss was in trouble, performances of the opera were cancelled after the third presentation, and Zweig fled abroad, to die by his own hand seven years later, depressed and disgusted at his fellow men.

Gradually, as the war began to turn against Germany, her rulers hardened their attitudes to people who, like Strauss, were not one hundred per cent pro-Nazi. Strauss was saved the embarrassment of being forced to join the Nazi Party against his better judgement by his Jewish connections, but he began to suffer real hardship and cruel treatment as conditions became crucial in the Third Reich. His title as head of the Reichsmusikkammer was taken away, his passport was confiscated and he was prevented from going to Switzerland for imperative cures. His family were not allowed to shop at normal places, were actively insulted when they went out of the house, and, had it not been for some diplomacy on Strauss's part with the local Gauleiter, might easily have been transported. Was this the way to treat the family of the 'pro-Nazi' composer whose works may not be performed in Israel even today?

Outwardly, he was a broken man when the war ended; he imagined that his music would never be played again anywhere. Yet the very nation which had sequestered his fortune in 1914 was the first to welcome him back, cleared of any Nazi taint so far as the Western Allies were concerned. The concerts of his music in London, sponsored by Sir Thomas Beecham—who had introduced Strauss's operas to London in 1910—did a great deal towards rehabilitating him in the public mind.

What upset Strauss more than anything was the destruction of four great German and Austrian opera-houses, where his works had first been heard and frequently been played since. The terrible losses which Germany suffered under the Nazi flag were a fearful blow to any German patriot, but especially to one as old as Strauss, who remembered the peacefulness that had existed there before 1914.

√ Strauss died painlessly in September 1949, unaware that his music was going to be played far more than ever before, that his estate would be worth more than in his lifetime, and that immense interest in him and in his compositions would follow. The opening of opera-houses to the general public, through government subsidies, rather than to society audiences as previously, the emergence of long-playing records and tape-recordings, and to a far lesser but not insignificant extent the omnipresence of television have all contributed in the post-war world to the dissemination of music, which has included Strauss's music in great quantities. Music is now the property of everybody, not the prerogative of the rich; nor is it confined to the concert-hall as it was before the first quarter of this century.

Strauss saw more changes in his eighty-five years than can be imagined except by his contemporaries—and there are not many of them left. Those years may be divided into three distinct eras: 1864–1914, when Strauss was at his height as man, as composer and as musician; 1914–45, the double-war period, when he was in decline; and 1945–9, which one might expect to be a moment of impotent silence before death, but when in fact he produced some of his loveliest compositions in a kind of inspirational twilight of old age. The much overused phrase 'indian summer' has been applied to these years of Strauss's life, and the balmy warmth which it evokes is for once very apt.

As an epitaph in music to the destruction of the Munich Opera House, Strauss composed his *Metamorphosen*, a chamber work for twenty-three solo strings, based on the funeral march in the slow movement of Beethoven's Third Symphony. It is possibly the saddest piece of music ever written, and it lasts some twenty-six minutes, perhaps a little on the long side despite its beauty.

The other works of this period, not sad at all but filled with the calmness and gaiety of youth, include: a second sonatina for wind instruments; a published version of the *Waltz: Munich*, but with an ending in keeping with the state of that city at the time; a new suite from *Der Rosenkavalier*, based on themes from Acts I and II; an oboe concerto of great fragrance and sweetness; a duet concertino for clarinet and bassoon with string orchestra and harp; and then four songs.

If I seem to emphasize these latter works of Strauss in contrast to the works of his maturity, it is only to lend weight to the argument that he was not played out in what I have called his second period of composition. In fact, at the end of those years, in 1942, he produced the opera *Capriccio*, which is fit to be set alongside his best stage-works for inspiration and good-natured humour, for luxury of sound and understanding of singers—for it is an opera *about* opera and singers. But during the remainder of these years, though he was outwardly going about his job of composing and conducting as usual and directing the musical affairs of Germany, inwardly he had shrivelled up. It needed the sense of a rebirth of Germany to revitalize him, and with the horror of everything he knew destroyed, coupled with the relief of knowing that those he held most dear were saved, he was over the worst and began composing again truly from the heart.

It is rare for a composer to recapture in old age anything like the tone of voice of his youth—indeed, one calls to mind only two who did so in their different ways: Verdi and Strauss. In Strauss's case one can only regret most deeply the two events which had the most damaging effects upon him as a composer: Hofmannsthal's insistence on leading him against his wishes; and the outbreak of the 1914 War. Had he been able to retire to Garmisch as he intended, with Hofmannsthal as his *obedient* librettist, the course of musical Europe would almost certainly have been changed. But this is only speculation: as it was, Strauss 'lost' twenty-eight composing years, but returned to the mood of his youth with truly nineteenth-century works, ending, as he had begun, with a song.

Strauss as Composer and Interpreter

There is a theory—a distinctly purist theory—that the lieder of Strauss are not *strict* lieder at all, the argument here being that in the lied music and words are—must be—of equal status. In the case of Strauss's lieder, the music is completely dominant, and in all but a few cases the poems which he chose to set are of inferior stuff. I suggest that critics who take this line should turn to Schubert for a moment: they will find that he too set some fairly poor poetry from time to time, and that there are plenty of his songs in which the music is far and away superior to the words which brought it into being. Goethe and Schiller may for the most part be above reproach, but is it reasonable to expect that every one of Schubert's 638 songs was based on a poetic masterpiece?

Even so, the argument is valid in the general sense that most of the poems were able to stand alone before the music further ennobled and enriched them. Schubert's art was an extension of the *Volkslied*: he extended its simple harmonies to make a new genre. So must every composer endeavour if he is to achieve a lasting place as a strong link in the musical heritage of his nation.

Strauss was no exception. His lieder, though often with piano accompaniment, were invariably visualized and composed with an orchestral support for the voice. This is very evident when we listen carefully to the pianist, whose part then appears that of somebody tackling an orchestral reduction at the keyboard. So he is, in a manner of speaking. Strauss's song 'Die heiligen drei Könige aus Morgenland', opus 56, no. 6, to the poem by Heinrich Heine, is a particular case in point. It was published in 1906 as the last song in a set of six, yet the piano score indicates a trumpet part in a total of six bars at the end of the song where there are thirty-one bars of postlude after the voice has finished. The orchestral version of 'Die heiligen drei Könige' was published at the same time as the set of songs to which it purports to belong, and the whole question which it poses seems to me to be self-answering. As this particular set of songs is full of interests in all kinds of directions, I shall be dwelling on it later.* In this case, Strauss's 'piano reduction' (for that is all it is) was the best way of completing the group of songs he had ready to make up the set.

In Schubert's case no song at all was orchestrated by the composer; that other people have made scores to fit the 'Ave Maria', and others, means nothing, for Schubert thought only in terms of voice and piano, and his two operas show how ill at ease he appeared when having to consider an orchestra to accompany his voices—ill at ease, that is, compared with such masters of the orchestral–vocal techniques as Strauss.

Thus the argument that rejects Strauss as a lieder composer stresses his closer affinity with the orchestra as accompanying instrument, in contrast to Schubert's closer affinity with the piano, traditionally the *only* support to the voice in lieder. And indeed, Strauss's contribution to the lied was in this very aspect, broadening its scope with the rich colours characteristic of his orchestral writing throughout. If we were to leave Strauss where his works for the piano ended, there would be little of his life to consider; but in accepting his large output of lieder (albeit only a third of Schubert's in number) we can accept his contribution to German song.

I draw these parallels with Schubert because he was undeniably the greatest master of the lied; but in doing so I point to Richard Strauss's unique place as an opera composer who—to use his own phrase—'kept his hand in' by writing for the voice in another medium. All the same, it was still generally for the operatic voice. Dedications and other knowledge we have of the interpreters of his songs indicate that they were primarily opera singers: his wife, Pauline; the celebrated bass Paul Knüpfer; the baritone Heinrich Schlusnus; and, much later on, Elisabeth Schumann.

Elisabeth Schumann is perhaps an exception because, although she sang a great deal on the opera stage, her voice was light, with great purity, clarity and power. It is even true to say that it had something of the quality of a boy's voice,

* See p. 108.

something of the beauty and innocence usually heard from the male treble only. Strauss chose Mme Schumann as the ideal interpreter of his lieder, and his opus 68 was composed with her voice in mind. (This was when Frau Strauss had retired from professional singing, in about 1918.)

Strauss was always happiest when composing for the soprano voice. He wrote several lieder for basses, but he was seldom sympathetic towards tenors. The poems he chose to set were not unfamiliar to his contemporaries in this field, and reference to Appendix D will show how they were often inspired to set the same words, the same poems which must have been fashionable and popular in Germany at the time. One cannot help noticing that these contemporary composers (and lesser ones, it must be added) set them after Strauss had done so, and in every case the Strauss setting is the one which has survived. Who, I wonder, has heard of Reger's 'Traum durch die Dämmerung', Pfitzner's 'Der Arbeitsmann', or Lassen's 'Allerseelen'? They may have enjoyed a vogue but they are unknown today.*

I do not mean to suggest that Strauss chose his poets or his poems with any particular clarity or distinction. The bulk of the poems are frankly out of step in their 'message' with the last quarter of the twentieth century, and when read without Strauss's musical clothing seem almost devoid of interest. Moreover, they are immensely 'old-fashioned' in a Victorian sense, but this is not surprising since the first of Strauss's lieder is now over a hundred years old and has an aura of age about it. They belong in the nineteenth century as Strauss himself seems to, though he lived for more than half his life in the twentieth.

So far I have referred generally to 'songs' or 'lieder', without distinguishing between those with piano and those with orchestral accompaniment (apart from one reference to opus 56, no. 6). Strauss, in titling his songs, distinguished between *Lied*, *Gesang*† and *Gedicht*‡, the last being merely a complimentary transfer of the written to the musical poem. *Gesang* applies

* Though Lassen's 'Allerseelen' was once well enough known to be recorded by Mme Kirkby-Lunn, Franz Völker and Emmy Bettendorf at different times.

† Opp. 43 and 77. ‡ Opp. 10, 21, 22 and 46.

elsewhere more accurately to the larger and orchestrated work. One must not fall into the trap of thinking that Strauss named the *Vier letzte Lieder* himself—he did not; yet in giving them this title, Dr Ernst Roth (Strauss's last publisher) must have been aware of the significance of the noun, and the significance of all Strauss's orchestrated songs in their relationship to the lied proper. I feel that the *Four Last Songs* are well named *Lieder*, and that one of Strauss's most important contributions to German lieder has been in their extension through the brain of a pre-eminently orchestrally minded composer towards a wider and more ample horizon.

One especially interesting aspect of Strauss's lieder which continually emerges is their total remoteness from the events which were going on round the composer. Thus the turbulent period which embraced *Salome* and *Elektra* finds no echo in the few lieder composed during this time; two world wars leave no scars in song; nor do we find any discarded bits and pieces from opera used up in accompaniments to lieder. Strauss's composition of lieder was a part of his life remote from anything else; so, in certain respects, was his accompanying of them.

We do not know for certain when he first began to accompany singers of his own works at the piano, but we do know that he built up this art into a formidable accomplishment, and that for over twenty years he and his wife gave numerous important recitals all over Germany. It appears, too, that in all these she was the dominating personality. As time went on and she had trouble with her teeth—something of which she was acutely conscious—Frau Pauline's dresses became more and more voluminous, her scarves and fans more extravagant, and her actions bigger and bigger in keeping. Even if there was a piano postlude to a song, she began to expect applause immediately her own contribution was at an end, and even moved over to cover Strauss from view. That he put up with this behaviour was all part of a domestic balance which is another story, but that he did bear with her in all sorts of awkward circumstances and scenes of her contrivance is witness to his great love for his wife. They understood each other completely, and consequently their lieder recitals—despite the occasional odd happening—must have been extraordinary examples of an almost unanimous interpretation by two people entirely at one with each other. Add to this the fact that the pianist was also the composer, and we can only lament the absence of any recordings of these performances.

Strauss is known to have varied his piano accompaniments from one recital to the next, sometimes furnishing elaborate and personal quotations according to his mood or even marking a special phrase for a friend in the audience. So it is a little disappointing—though understandable in the circumstances—to find that in the very few recordings which Strauss has left of himself as accompanist he adheres strictly to his own notes as written, and offers model though by no means exceptional examples of how he played 'straight'.*

There may be several reasons why Strauss allowed himself to make improvisations while he was accompanying, but certainly it was principally to overcome boredom. Some of his songs, as already described, met with such acclaim that it became almost painful for him to hear them in later years, especially when they were indifferently sung. Another reason lies in Strauss's mental processes, which were always at work in composing, no matter what he was apparently thinking about at the time.

Strauss was not a pianist of the first rank. He always admitted that his left hand was weak, due to lack of emphasis on it from his teachers and lack of concentration in his own practice. It never allowed him to play the solo part in his *Burleske*, and perhaps the lesson he learnt here persuaded him to write his lieder accompaniments to be within the scope of a good pianist rather than the meat for a virtuoso.

In his programme-building of lieder recitals we know that Strauss eschewed the 'straight-through-the-group' idea for a carefully mixed selection of songs across the years, more notable for contrast in mood and key than in opus number or poet. For example, in building a lieder recital to be given in Brunswick at the end of October 1908, Strauss plans the evening with five groups of songs thus:

* 'Breit' über mein Haupt' and 'Morgen!' with the tenor Robert Hutt; 'Heimkehr' and 'Ich liebe dich', 'Ruhe, meine Seele' and 'Zueignung', 'Geheimnis' and 'Die Nacht', all with the baritone Heinrich Schlusnus.

I	'Zueignung'	op. 10, no. 1
	'Du meines Herzens Krönelein'	op. 21, no. 2
	'Ach Lieb, ich muss nun scheiden'	op. 21, no. 3
	'All mein Gedanken'	op. 21, no. 1
	'Ständchen'	op. 17, no. 2
II	'Ich trage meine Minne'	op. 32, no. 1
	'Ein Obdach gegen Sturm und Regen'	op. 46, no. 1
	'Freundliche Vision'	op. 48, no. 1
	'Jung Hexenlied'	op. 39, no. 2
III	'Himmelsboten zu Liebchens Himmelbett'	op. 32, no. 5
	'Morgen!'	op. 27, no. 4
	'Die heiligen drei Könige'	op 56, no. 6
	'In goldener Fülle'	op. 49, no. 2
IV	'Das Rosenband'	op. 36, no. 1
	'Wiegenlied'	op. 41, no. 1
	'Mit deinen blauen Augen'	op. 56, no. 4
	'Heimliche Aufforderung'	op. 27, no. 3
V	'Gefunden'	op. 56, no. 1
	'Ich schwebe'	op. 48, no. 2
	'Traum durch die Dämmerung'	op. 29, no. 1
	'Cäcilie'	op. 27, no. 2

At the time when this recital was planned and given Strauss had reached his peak as a lieder composer. Between 1882 and 1906 he had 108 lieder for voice and piano to his credit, and one may reasonably assume that this selection of twenty-one of them gives some indication of which were most acceptable, which Strauss and his wife liked performing best, and which were most likely to profit him when they were sung. One thing that stands out in the selection is the absence of any humorous song.

By 1908 Strauss had stopped composing lieder altogether and had begun to devote his whole creative time to operas—though lieder recitals still took up a considerable part of his conducting itineraries. He now lacked the time to search for poems which would 'set themselves'. But it must not be assumed that he had lost his taste for this very intimate branch of music: if the opportunity for a recital occurred while he was planning his conducting tours, Strauss accepted it, and very often took his wife with him, providing the recital was to take place not too far away. Thus he kept up the partnership, which in fact continued until towards the end of the First World War.

When it finally ended, Strauss found in Elisabeth Schumann the ideal interpreter of his songs, and he composed for her the set opus 68, the Brentano lieder, which they took to America in 1921. Between the end of October 1921 and 1 January 1922 Strauss conducted a great number of concerts in the United States, but he also gave lieder recitals with Mme Schumann. (Frau Strauss stayed behind in Garmisch, but sent Franz Strauss with his father as chaperon.)

This was probably the last tour of any length in which Strauss acted as accompanist at the keyboard. Certainly in the twenties and thirties and up to the beginning of the Second World War he seemed more at home conducting orchestrated versions of his songs, and as late as 15 September 1944 he interpolated four of them into an orchestral concert, when Julius Patzak sang 'Ständchen', 'Morgen!', 'Ich trage meine Minne' and 'Heimliche Aufforderung'.

3 *The Early Songs*

We do not know for certain how many songs Richard Strauss wrote between 1870 and 1882; but we have concrete evidence of thirty-six. These are known collectively as the *Jugendlieder*, but since they overlap the first two groups of what are reckoned as mature lieder, and four more occur between 1882 and 1886, the collection, which has never before been classified in chronological order, needs some explanation.

The first composition by Richard Strauss was a song—his 'Weihnachtslied', to which I have referred earlier.* Simple piano works and songs followed, until in 1876 Strauss wrote his first orchestral piece to receive publication. This has since been known as opus 1, although at a much earlier date Strauss was giving his compositions opus numbers of two series, many of which he later discarded, reallocating numbers in the light of his maturing skill and the search for an individual style.

Although Strauss was meticulous in the way he preserved letters and manuscripts, work-books and diaries, he parted company with a number of early songs without, it seems, making copies. Twelve of them went to his aunt Johanna Pschorr in Munich with his fond dedication, and were never published. Max Steinitzer, who wrote the first biography of Strauss in 1908, saw them (presumably at Strauss's sister's house in Munich) round about the turn of the century; he gave numbers to them in a list of his own, described them (though not in much detail), and passed on to what he considered, rightly enough, to be more important compositions. So a comparison of the titles in Steinitzer's list with copies and originals in the Strauss Archive in Garmisch reveals a number of missing manuscripts, of which all we know today is what Steinitzer has said about them. Of course there may have been other songs which Steinitzer never saw, and which also disappeared: we do not know, and further speculation in this

* See p. 1.

direction is merely idle. Since the publication of three sketches for unfinished songs* we are probably now in possession of all the information that there is.

Steinitzer's list has been augmented by four songs which he never saw, and these will be found in the chronological list of existing *Jugendlieder* in Appendix B. This will not coincide with a full list, which would show the lost songs and sketches and works which do not belong to this book, but is adequate for present purposes.

Apart from the 'Weihnachtslied' there are two others of special interest. 'Der Spielmann und sein Kind' is a long and elaborate song, if not a *scena*, of nearly 250 bars, which resembles in conception the much later orchestral songs of opus 44, as well as showing some similarity to Schubert's 'Der Erlkönig'. 'Der Spielmann' is of special interest because it was the first of all Strauss's songs to be orchestrated. It exists in both orchestral and piano versions, though only the piano one has been published. One can only guess, at present, how the thirteen-year-old composer tackled the stormy story with the larger palette. This song was composed between 15 and 28 February 1878, and it is immensely significant that Strauss was already thinking in orchestral terms.

Another song of consequence that cannot strictly be called a lied is 'Ein Alphorn', for soprano, piano and horn. I will deal later with this song, which is unique in conception in Strauss's output.

Opus 10, the *Letzte Blätter* of Hermann von Gilm, is the generally acknowledged start to the mature lieder, although the three lieder shown in Appendix B as J29, J31 and J37 are sometimes found as a set between opp. 10 and 15, without an opus number. Strauss's East German biographer, Ernst Krause,† gives the date of these three songs as 1883–4, but we now know that this is incorrect. On the completion of the third one, 'Rote Rosen', Strauss put them all together and sent them to Lotte Speyer, with his dedication to her over the new one, on 19 October 1883. Subsequently known as *Three Love Songs for Voice and Piano* they were placed in the order 'Rote Rosen', 'Die erwachte Rose' and 'Begegnung' (Strauss's own

* *Nachlese* (Boosey & Hawkes, 1968).

† *Richard Strauss: the Man and his Work* (trs. J. Coombs), (Collet's, 1965).

title for Gruppe's poem). The three songs became the property of Lotte Speyer's niece, Charlotte A. Kleiss, in America, who gave permission for them to be published there in 1958. They were performed at the Carnegie Hall, New York, by Elisabeth Schwarzkopf and Gerald Moore on 30 November 1958. Whether Lotte Speyer ever sang them herself in the last century is not known.

Only one other of the *Jugendlieder* is dedicated to a singer and may thus have been performed: this is 'Waldesgesang', to a poem by Emanuel Geibel, which bears the inscription above the song: *Fräulein C. Meysenheym, Singer at the Royal Opera,* with grateful thanks.* It is dated 9 April 1879: a precocious effort for a boy of not quite fifteen.

The songs J35, J36 and J38–40, although coming between opp. 10 and 15 in date order, are not generally accepted as part of the mature canon, and must still be classified as youthful efforts: as Strauss did not give them a place in one of his earlier groups, it seems evident that he did not regard them as mature either. So they have been pushed into the background, although they help to form a bridge between the *Jugendlieder* and the opus-numbered songs and to join them tightly together.

I shall later single out one or two of the *Jugendlieder* which either fit into my scheme of things or else have special merit. However, I propose to start my description of the lieder with the first one Strauss ever composed: the 'Weihnachtslied', of which I have already said something above.† For a small child who could not even write in the words of Schubart's poem, it is no mean achievement. First of all it is not in C major, as one might expect, but in E major. The accents are all absolutely right, and possibly the only feeble aspect is the left hand; but at 'sanftem Himmelswind' there is a perfectly logical modulation to G sharp minor; and the whole shape of the *Liedchen* is decided by the words, which do not allow a repetition or development of the musical phrase which ends on 'Wiegenlied-', for there is only '-chen für' before the valedic-

* *K. b. Hofopernsängerin*, a title bestowed on certain singers by the Kaiser, which counted as more of an honour than the present *Kammersängerin*, the nearest approach to it.

† See pp. 1 & 20.

tory three words, which Strauss puts in two bars. But in these two bars there are two further signs that a real composer is at work: the E sharp in the bass and the suspension are far further on in musical thought than even the most precocious six-year-old might hope to achieve.

Schlaf' wohl du Himmelsknabe du,	Sleep well, you heavenly Boy,
schlaf' wohl du süsses Kind;	sleep well, you sweet Child,
dich fächeln Engelein in Ruh,	angels fan you to rest,
mit sanftem Himmelswind.	with a gentle breeze from above.
Wir armen Hirten singen dir	We poor shepherds sing you
ein herzlich Wiegenliedchen für,	a loving little lullaby,
schlafe, Himmelskindlein, schlafe.	sleep, little heavenly child, sleep.

The set of eight Lieder, opus 10, from poems by Hermann von Gilm, is always regarded as the true beginning of Strauss's lieder-writing career; although, as we have seen, it was prefaced by many early songs in what might be described as the apprentice class, and not a few others of some merit. It is as if Strauss suddenly found a formula when he embarked on the first song in this set, 'Zueignung'—Strauss's title for Gilm's untitled poem, the only one of the set which was not taken from the collection called *Letzte Blätter*. Strauss's formula was immensely successful.

Ja, du weisst es, teure Seele, dass ich fern von dir mich quäle, Liebe macht die Herzen krank, habe Dank.	Yes, you know it well, dear heart, that I cannot bear to be parted far from you. Love makes hearts sick, I am grateful!
Einst hielt ich, der Freiheit Zecher, hoch den amethysten Becher und du segnetest den Trank, habe Dank.	Once when I was carefree, carousing, I held the cup of amethyst aloft and you blessed the drink, I am grateful!
Und beschworst darin die Bösen, bis ich, was ich nie gewesen, heilig, heilig an's Herz dir sank, habe Dank.	You banished the evil spirits until I was what I have never been, holy—and holy, I sank upon your breast, I am grateful!

This song was originally composed in C major and is marked (as indeed the whole set is) *Für hohe Singstimme mit Pianofortebegleitung*. Since this does not expressly mean 'for soprano voice', it is not so surprising—though unusual for Strauss—to find that he described the set as 'real tenor songs'.

The setting of 'Zueignung' is a simple one, though it bears the mark of an exceptional mind. The most notable aspect is in the quaver rest at the third and fifth bars and on the first beat of the melody. The verses are exactly alike for the first four bars only: after this on the first occasion a cadence in A minor prefaces a long pause for the singer before the 'habe Dank'; the second time it moves into F major and 'habe Dank' comes more swiftly, as if deeply felt; and then for the last time, after an accompaniment thicker, lusher and more impassioned than before, we are taken quickly via F major, E minor and A minor, with almost two bars' rest in the voice-part while the accompaniment resolves itself into C major and its seventh for a valedictory 'habe Dank'. Strauss never wrote the music for a song as if it were a hymn: even though—as was usual—the poem was set out in stanzas, the song was through-composed and became a musical entity, emphasizing the thought behind the poem which makes a shape of the whole.

The accompanying pattern to 'Zueignung' is a slow left hand in (mainly) octaves, supporting a right hand of triplets, with the first four (repetitive) bars of each of the poet's stanzas emphasizing the quaver rests.

There is an orchestral version of the song by the conductor–composer Robert Heger, dating from 1933. It had Strauss's approval to the extent that he often conducted it himself at orchestral concerts. Nevertheless, by way of a token of—somewhat delayed—thanks to the soprano Viorica Ursuleac for her portrayal of Helena in the revised *Die ägyptische Helena* in 1933, Strauss orchestrated 'Zueignung' himself and altered the words in the last two lines to read 'du wunderbare Helena, habe Dank'. This was in 1940. The extra words needed special attention, and Strauss was obliged to insert a 3/2 bar for 'Herz dir sank' as well as a different shape for the finale. This version of 'Zueignung' is too personal to be sung by anybody else, except as a curiosity; while any attempt to edit Strauss's score to fit the original words seems totally unjustified. In the orchestral field, Heger's score will probably remain the version to be performed.

'Ständchen' is the second song in Strauss's opus 17, a set of six after poems by von Schack composed between 1885 and 1887. The words of the poem may be unsophisticated, but Strauss brings to his setting a lightness of touch which altogether transforms the banal words into a masterpiece. This is the first of a handful of Strauss's early songs to become immensely popular in their own time, as well as continuing to charm listeners today.

Mach' auf, mach' auf, doch leise, mein Kind,	Open the door, open the door, but quietly my love,
um keinen vom Schlummer zu wecken.	so as not to awaken anyone from sleep.
Kaum murmelt der Bach, kaum zittert im Wind	The brook scarcely murmurs, the breeze scarcely stirs
ein Blatt an den Büschen und Hecken.	a leaf on the bushes and hedgerows.
Drum leise, mein Mädchen, dass nichts sich regt,	Gently, then, my darling, so that nothing stirs,
nur leise die Hand auf die Klinke gelegt.	put your hand gently on the latch.
Mit Tritten wie Tritte der Elfen so sacht,	With steps as light as the elves' steps
um über die Blumen zu hüpfen.	when they skip over the flowers,
Flieg' leicht hinaus in die Mondscheinnacht,	fly lightly out into the moonlit night,
zu mir in den Garten zu schlüpfen.	slip out and join me in the garden.
Rings schlummern die Blüten am rieselnden Bach	Around us the flowers sleep by the rippling brook
und duften im Schlaf, nur die Liebe ist wach.	and breathe their fragrance in sleep; only love is awake.
Sitz' nieder, hier dämmert's geheimnisvoll	Sit here in the mysterious twilight
unter den Lindenbäumen,	under the linden trees,
die Nachtigall uns zu Häupten soll	the nightingale above our heads shall
von uns'ren Küssen träumen	dream of our kisses
und die Rose, wenn sie am Morgen erwacht,	and the rose, when it wakens in the morning,
hoch glühn von den Wonneschauern der Nacht.	shall glow deeply from the night's ecstasy.

Strauss marks his setting *Vivace e dolce*; the song is in F sharp major and in 6/8–9/8 time. After the more ponderous nature of 'Zueignung', Strauss injects—by comparison—far more immediacy and a quiet yet insistent urgency. This is partly achieved by the quaver at the end of the first four bars of the vocal line (after the first, empty bar) followed by a dotted crotchet as the first beat of each of the next bars. He gives a feeling to the brook and the trees by making the singer draw out the words, emphasizing the murmuring and the half-movement respectively. It is the last two lines of each of the first two stanzas which go into 9/8 to accommodate the extra words. The first and second verse accompaniments are exactly the same, except where the sense needs different dynamic markings; but when we reach the third, where the lovers are together, the whole setting changes. The piano accompaniment does not alter from its two groups of six semiquavers to the bar, but it achieves an interesting modulation for the poem's climax in D, a far cry from the original key of F sharp. A quick return to F sharp brings a triumphant ending for 'hoch glühn', each word taking a whole bar, to come down peacefully to the final word 'Nacht', followed only by a piano coda in 9/8 ending with flourishing, quaver-length broken chords.

'Wozu noch, Mädchen' is the first song in the set opus 19 which Strauss composed in 1885 to von Schack's *Lotosblätter*, and it is one of his earliest essays into a kind of delicacy which manages to avoid all sentimentality. The song is the puzzled plea of a young man to a girl, asking why she won't stop pretending and admit that she loves him. Strauss manages to convey in his music the question-mark that is clearly in the young man's voice all the time, and with which the song ends.

Wozu noch, Mädchen, soll es frommen,	What good, my child, do you think it can do
dass du vor mir Verstellung übst?	to keep your secret from me?
Heiss' froh das neue Glück willkommen	Greet your new happiness gladly,
und sag' es offen, dass du liebst!	And say openly that you are in love.
An deines Busens höherm Schwellen,	By the deeper heaving of your breast,
dem Wangenrot, das kommt und geht,	the rosy blush, that comes and goes,
ward dein Geheimnis von den Quellen,	your secret has long since been discovered

den Blumengeistern längst erspäht;
die Wogen murmeln's in den Grotten,
es flüstert's leis' der Abendwind,
wo du vorbeigehst, hörst du's spotten:
Wir wissen es seit lange, Kind!
Kind!
Wozu noch, Mädchen, soll es frommen,
dass du vor mir Verstellung übst?

by the fountains and flower-spirits;
the waves murmur it in the caves,
the evening wind whispers it softly,
As you pass by, you hear them mocking:
'We have known it for a long time, child!'
Child!
What good then can it do
to keep your secret from me?

The hesitating accompaniment which underlines the awkwardness of the question continues until the words 'du liebst'. Then the singer becomes a little more assured, and he is supported by six full *ostinato* quavers to the bar, hammering out the reasoning behind his plea. On the word 'liebst' there is a sudden key-change into A major, and this little phrase (*x*) is introduced for the first time:

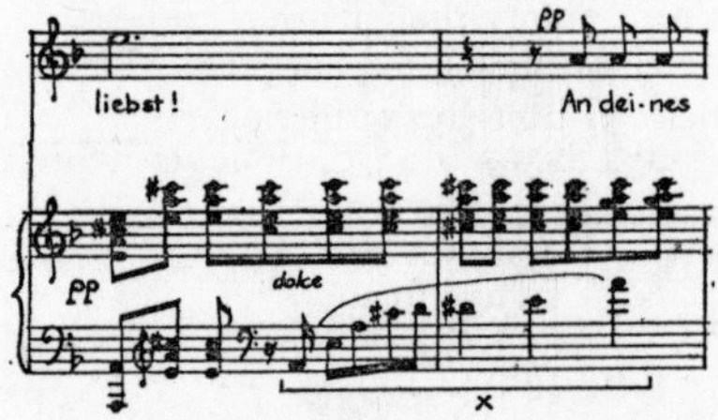

This seems to imply some optimism: by facing her and putting the question straight, he will surely persuade her to answer him. At all events he sounds courageous for the moment. The mocking is clear in 'hörst du's spotten', with derisive and slippery little grace-chords in the accompaniment, and now she *must* answer him.

But no. We are returned to the same, hesitant approach as at the beginning of the song, followed by the chord of B flat major seventh, perplexed and unanswered, and the reverse of the upward-moving motif, now drooping disconsolately. He is not getting an answer—perhaps she is so young that she is bashful; perhaps she is old enough to know when she is teasing him!

Furthermore, the most ambiguous of all chords, the diminished seventh, underlines it as it underlies the situation. A final semiquaver run finishes on F in alt, but not in the *key* of F.

Strauss has managed to pack into this short song a feeling and a mood to match or even to anticipate every change in the young man's approach to the unresponsive girl. While von Schack has described it neatly, Strauss has made a little masterpiece out of it. Furthermore, it is ideally pianistic. It is a true lied.

The third song in this quiet, contemplative and charming set (unlike any other, since the mood does not vary much from song to song) is 'Schön sind, doch kalt, die Himmelssterne'. It has an accompaniment very much after the style of Schubert, and in a manner which we shall encounter again. Strauss also introduced it into his operas.* The song is in 3/8 time, and begins and ends firmly in B flat major.

Schön sind, doch kalt, die Himmelssterne,	Beautiful but cold are the stars of heaven,
die Gaben karg, die sie verleih'n;	empty the gifts they provide;
für einen deiner Blicke, gerne	in return for one look from you
hin geb' ich ihren gold'nen Schein.	I'd gladly sacrifice all their golden light.
Getrennt, so dass wir ewig darben,	When we are apart, for ever hungering,
nur führen sie im Jahreslauf	they bring no more in the course of the seasons
den Herbst mit seinen Ährengarben,	than autumn with its corn-sheaves
des Frühlings Blütenpracht herauf;	and spring with its splendour of blossom.
doch deine Augen, o, der Segen	But your eyes brim over
des ganzen Jahres quillt überreich	with the abundance of the whole year
aus ihnen stets als milder Regen,	as with gentle rain,
die Blüte und die Frucht zugleich.	the blossom and the fruit all at once.

* The other songs are op. 21, no. 2, and op. 56, no. 4. In the operas the final duet in *Der Rosenkavalier* and the trio of nymphs in *Ariadne auf Naxos* are the more obvious instances. See pp. 32–3.

The song begins in a definite B flat, moving into A flat, then returning until the sad word 'getrennt', when we are in B flat minor; thence to F minor and thereabouts until the sudden and wonderful chord which occurs in the bar with 'ihnen':

Thence there is a return to the home key for a gentle descent after 'Regen' and the valedictory phrase, sung quietly and peacefully.

'Wie sollten wir geheim sie halten' is the fourth song in opus 19. It bubbles with energy, an energy which stems from the left hand, though there are often triplet chords in both hands, twelve to the bar. This extensive movement hardly ceases for the whole song, which achieves an excitement, rather than a restlessness; and this is something which Strauss has succeeded in doing that raises the whole feeling of the song, rather than letting it remain breathless and exhausting to hear.

Wie sollten wir geheim sie halten,
die Seligkeit, die uns erfüllt?
Nein, bis in seine tiefsten Falten
sei allen unser Herz enthüllt.

Why should we keep it to ourselves,
the happiness that fills us both?
No, down to their deepest recesses
let our hearts be openly revealed to all.

Wenn zwei in Liebe sich gefunden,
geht Jubel hin durch die Natur,
in längern wonnevollen Stunden
legt sich der Tag auf Wald und Flur.

When two people are in love,
great is the rejoicing throughout Nature,
through prolonged, ecstatic hours
the day spreads over woods and meadows.

Selbst auch der Eiche morschem Stamm,	Even from the oaktree's rotting trunk,
die ein Jahrtausend überlebt,	which has outlived a thousand years,
steigt neu des Wipfels grüne Flamme	a new green growth starts from the top
und rauscht von Jugendlust durchbebt.	and rustles, alive with the zest of youth.
Zu höherm Glanz und Dufte brechen	In greater splendour and fragrance
die Knospen auf beim Glück der Zwei	the buds burst open at the lovers' joy,
und süsser rauscht es in den Bächen,	and the brooks more sweetly murmur
und reicher blüht und reicher glänzt der Mai.	and May more richly blooms and more brightly shines.
Wie sollten wir geheim sie halten, usw.	Why should we keep it to ourselves, etc.

The first verbal phrase is made extremely gripping and thrilling by two *portamenti* for the singer, both downwards, on 'Wie sollten' and on 'geheim'. It is one of Strauss's most jubilantly joyful love songs, bringing into the poem—in the true lieder tradition—mention of nature: woods, fields, trees, buds, the merrily flowing stream, and the bright air of May. Here is a truly German song, with German lovers revelling in their wonderful countryside. Both poet and composer must have had the same feeling in order to render it into words and music with such conviction, and the result is an admirable achievement.

'Du meines Herzens Krönelein' is second in the set opus 21, and is to words by Felix Dahn. It dates from 1887, and is in the key of G flat major, a steady *andante* in 2/4 time.

Du meines Herzens Krönelein,	You are the very crown of my heart,
du bist von laut'rem Golde,	you are of pure gold;
wenn andere daneben sein,	when others are set beside you
dann bist du noch viel holder.	then you seem even more lovely.

Die andern tun so gern gescheut, du bist gar sanft und stille, dass jedes Herz sich dein erfreut, dein Glück ist's, nicht dein Wille.	The others like to show off, you are so gentle and quiet that every heart rejoices in you— it is your charm, not your design.
Die andern suchen Lieb' und Gunst mit tausend falschen Worten, du ohne Mund- und Augenkunst bist wert an allen Orten.	The others may court love and favour with a thousand false words; you need no art of lip or eye to be adored everywhere.
Du bist, als wie die Ros' im Wald, sie weisst nichts von ihrer Blüte, doch jedem, der vorüberwallt, erfreut sie das Gemüte.	You are like the wild rose which is unaware of its blossom, but which delights the hearts of all who pass by.

There is a story told about this song by Alfred Orel, once Professor of Music at Vienna University, and sometime page-turner for Strauss at lieder recitals. Strauss had been accompanying his wife in this song one day, and Orel was listening to him improvising very quietly while applause was going on:

The very Schubertian figure which at once came into Strauss's mind is from the final duet for Sophie and Octavian in *Der Rosenkavalier*:

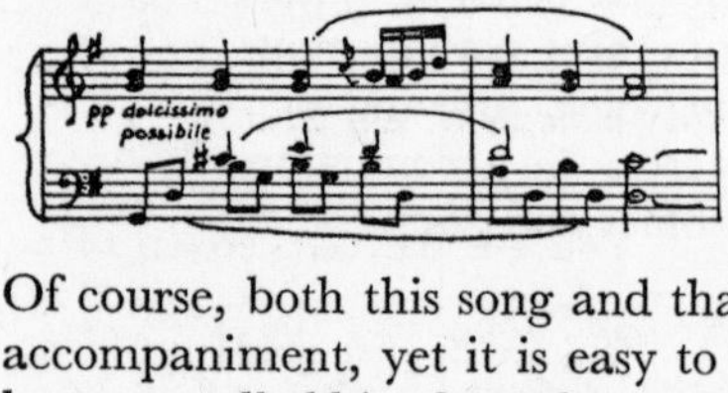

Of course, both this song and that duet have a Schubert-like accompaniment, yet it is easy to see how Strauss's mind can have propelled him from the one into the direction of the other. It may be that Strauss was indeed paying tribute to Schubert with the repeated use of this kind of accompanying figure—as for instance with the deliberate quotation from Schubert's 'Wiegenlied', D.498, for the trio of nymphs in *Ariadne*:

The songs in opus 21 are probably more pianistic than those which come later, which is perhaps why none was orchestrated by Strauss. Certainly those in the vein of Schubert conform more to true lieder than to the brand Strauss made his own, which have an orchestral feeling about them and are uncomfortable or just difficult on the piano.

One of the finest songs which Strauss ever wrote is 'Morgen!', opus 27, no. 4, composed in September 1894; the orchestral version followed in September 1897. John Henry Mackay's poem is successful because it creates a perfect atmosphere, not only by the words as they stand but also by what is behind the words, the heart of them. The chief beauty of the song lies in its simplicity, and in the repetition of the accompaniment, which leads us to sense an endless and preordained motion. Breaking into this—perhaps not breaking so much as floating—comes the voice, arriving on a G sharp when the song is in G. And across the accompaniment, across what it is saying, the singer comes and goes.

Und morgen wird die Sonne wieder scheinen	And tomorrow the sun will be shining again,
und auf dem Wege, den ich gehen werde,	and on the path that I shall take

wird uns, die Glücklichen, sie wieder einen	it will unite us once more in happiness,
inmitten dieser sonnenatmenden Erde . . .	in the midst of this sun-breathing earth . . .
und zu dem Strand, dem weiten, wogenblauen,	and to the shore, broad and blue-waved,
werden wir still und langsam niedersteigen,	we shall climb down, quietly and slowly;
stumm werden wir uns in die Augen schauen,	wordlessly we shall look into each other's eyes
und auf uns sinkt des Glückes stummes Schweigen. . . .	and upon us will descend the perfect silence of joy. . . .

Although the poem was written in two stanzas, each of four long lines, Strauss's setting changes direction altogether on the word 'Stumm' (at the beginning of the last line but one). A slow succession of semibreves brings the voice down through E flat and A flat to end on the leading note of the scale of G. So the song comes in on G sharp and goes out on F sharp, giving the impression that it hasn't really gone at all: that it is still near by.

When Strauss orchestrated 'Morgen!' three years later he preserved its fragility by using no woodwind, only three horns, a harp and strings. A solo violin doubles the top line of the accompaniment, but does not play at all from the word 'Stumm' until after the voice has ceased. There was once, incidentally, a bad habit of using a solo violin with the piano accompaniment to this song: there is no licence whatever for this, and I hope no respectable pianist would tolerate it today, though there have been several recordings made like this in the past with world-famous singers.

The harp takes all the triplet arpeggios, the solo violin takes the accompanying melody, while the other violins and violas sustain the inner parts with tied notes. Cellos and basses play only the first crotchet in each bar (apart from a one-bar phrase which cellos play in contrary motion twice). The full score is a model of refined thought and execution, and is the first published example of a conventional lied orchestrated by Strauss himself, so that his wife, the 'incomparable' interpreter of his songs, might include some of them at his orchestral concerts when he was conducting. In this same year, 1897,

Strauss orchestrated four more lieder,* making this a very important year in the reformation of the lied through his orchestration. He had already composed the four *Gesänge*, opus 33, which are specifically *not* lieder; though even before opus 33, he had composed an orchestral accompaniment—never published—for the Jugendlied 'Der Spielmann und sein Kind'.† Again the version with orchestra preceded the piano-accompanied version. 'Morgen!' is really the dawning of Strauss's career as an orchestrator of lieder first written for voice and piano alone, thus extending the scope and the power of the lied to this medium of which he was a master.

'Das Rosenband' is to a poem by Klopstock, in Strauss's catalogue opus 36, no. 1, dated 22 December 1897. Schubert also set this poem—in his list it is D280, one of the minor lieder dating from September 1817.

For Strauss to set a poem already beautifully composed by Schubert—of all men—is unique; and if Strauss knew the earlier setting he was not in the least influenced by it. Schubert's lied is in A flat and takes thirty-nine bars; Strauss's is in A major (according to the key-signature) and takes forty-four. Schubert's is very simply laid out and makes much play with A flat–A natural, D flat–D natural, G flat–G natural as if deliberately fluctuating between the keys of E flat–A flat–D flat: Strauss's is complicated and has enormously wide harmonic implications between A and C and suddenly to E flat, with thick, lush chords that tie down an otherwise light and frothy ambience.

Im Frühlingsschatten fand ich sie,	In the spring shade I found her;
da band ich sie mit Rosenbändern:	and tied her with rose-chains;
sie fühlt' es nicht und schlummerte.	she felt nothing, and slept on.

* 'Liebeshymnus' (see p. 47); 'Das Rosenband' (see below); 'Cäcilie' (see p. 60) and 'Meinem Kinde'.

† See p. 21.

Ich sah sie an; mein Leben hing mit diesem Blick an ihrem Leben: ich fühlt' es wohl und wusst' es nicht.	I gazed at her: my life hung on her life with this look; I felt it, and did not know it.
Doch lispelt' ich ihr sprachlos zu und rauschte mit den Rosenbändern: da wachte sie vom Schlummer auf.	But I whispered sounds into her ear and shook the rose-chains: then she awoke from sleep.
Sie sah mich an; ihr Leben hing mit diesem Blick an meinem Leben und um uns ward's Elysium.	She gazed at me: her life hung on my life with this look, and around us it was suddenly Paradise.

Seeing the repeated mirror-phrase ('my life hung on her life' . . . 'her life hung on my life') it is natural to expect that both Schubert and Strauss would have used the same musical phrase (each in his own manner) for the two occasions. Schubert did, exactly; and Strauss nearly did. Strauss had it the first time in E flat modulating to E, and the second in A modulating to D with the same melody. By the end of the second phrase he had arrived at the right take-off point for 'und um uns', which he exults in and repeats (though I find the three words ugly, strung together like this), before a long vocal cadenza on 'Elysium', taking the whole melody—and the lied—out of this world, as it were.

The Schubertians will, naturally, have none of Strauss's setting. *Their* lied surpasses it in Schubert's pacing of the word 'schlummerte' on three minims, likewise the phrases 'fühlt' es wohl' and 'wusst' es nicht', with crotchets, dotted crotchets and quavers round them. Of course, Schubert's utter simplicity and transparency are wonderful too; and while he repeats the melody exactly in the second stanza, his accompaniment varies completely, consisting the second time entirely of running quavers, often in contrary motion to the melody and only occasionally guiding the singer.

By comparison—and here it must end—Strauss's 'Das Rosenband' is extravagant. It even smacks of the Ariadne–

Bacchus duet, at the start: a lavish bar and a half of bravura modulation from A to E flat to C to the chord:

and back to A! As for the 'und um uns' phrase, Strauss repeats the words to great effect, while the final cadenza, as I have said, has nothing to equal it in any of his lieder—until the *Four Last Songs*.

Another feature of Strauss's song is the twelve upward octave leaps, hardly ever elsewhere to be encountered in his lieder. They add to the lightness, particularly in the vocal line.

'Das Rosenband' was orchestrated on the same day that the piano score was composed, so that we may take it that Strauss preferred the full version. This is scored for an unusual balance: 3 flutes and a piccolo, 2 oboes, 2 clarinets and bass clarinet, 2 bassoons, 2 horns and 36 strings (10, 10, 6, 6, 4). The piccolo starts with high trills while the second violins play trills in thirds, off the beat, four quavers to a bar; the violas execute wide arpeggios up and down in semiquavers and the cellos play in triplets. The movement and counter-movement in the strings can be imagined. At the famous phrase 'Ich sah sie an', it all settles down, only to resume its activity. The complementary 'Sie sah mich an' is quite differently scored, while a solo violin acts as a pendant to the voice in a cadenza-like coda.

The first song in opus 37, which dates from 1896–8, is called 'Glückes genug'. It is a serene little song, as its description (*Sehr ruhig*) indicates. It is in 4/8 time, in the key of F sharp major, and expresses the supreme happiness which comes from being one of a married partnership. This purity, which the poet Detlev von Liliencron expresses, is not only charming, and in character with the man who had a great admiration for women and consummated love, but it is the core of a moving poem.

Strauss gives the pianist big fistfuls of notes to play and wide broken chords to put down, thus achieving a marvellous change of key from E major (where the harmony has arrived easily enough from F sharp) to C sharp minor and then, in a moment of wonderment and silence from the singer, to D sharp major with the dominant sharpened a semitone. This is a famous Wagnerian chord which often occurs in the *Ring*, and Strauss repeats it to get the voice to C major. There is something very mature and assured about this Wagnerian colouring which altogether suits the song.

Wenn sanft du mir im Arme schliefst,	When you lay softly asleep in my arms,
ich deinen Atem hören konnte,	when I heard your breathing,
im Traum du meinen Namen riefst,	when you called my name in a dream,
um deinen Mund ein Lächeln sonnte,	when a smile stole round your mouth,
Glückes genug.	perfect joy!
Und wenn nach heissem, ernstem Tag	And when after the heat and passion of the day
du mir verscheuchtest schwere Sorgen,	you smoothed away my heavy cares,
wenn ich an deinem Herzen lag	when I lay beside you
und nicht mehr dachte an ein Morgen	and thought no longer of the morrow,
Glückes genug.	perfect joy!

The progression returns from C—innocently, and as if nothing has happened at all—to a cascade of B flat major sevenths, to an impertinent pivot enharmonically on C to E flat (B sharp–D sharp), to the seventh of the home key, and back to the tonic of F sharp major. It looks like this, and it is a very deft piece of Straussian modulation:

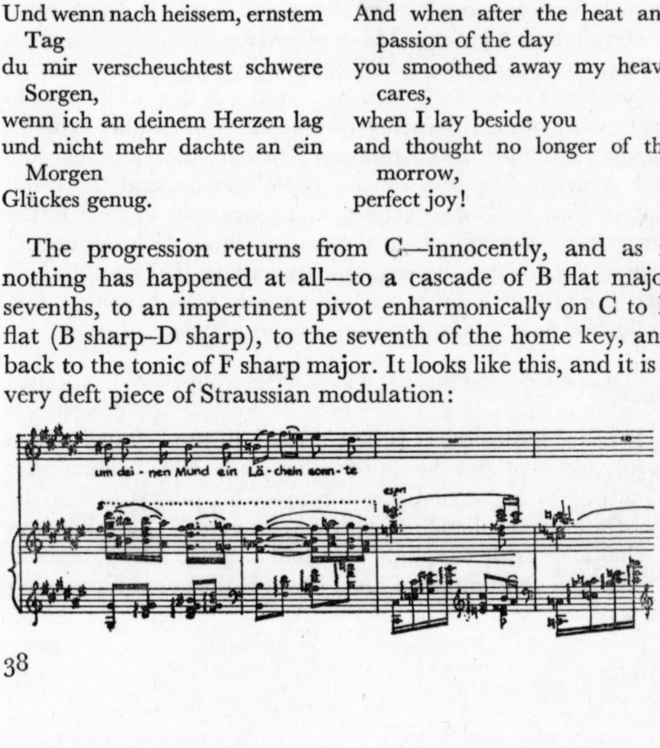

'Mein Auge' offers a wonderfully lush start. But after the first two bars it becomes more introspective and harder to follow; it is more difficult to understand what Strauss is getting at. At first it even seems that he is developing an intellectual exercise from the song, rather than giving way to the beauty of sound as, particularly, he had done in 'Das Rosenband'. But repeated hearing will dispel this idea, and it is the score of the orchestrated version which gives an immediate insight into the song.

'Mein Auge' first appeared in 1898 as op. 37, no. 4; the orchestrated version was completed in September 1933—the year of *Arabella*. Even so, despite the thirty-five years between the two versions, it is hard to believe that Strauss had ever thought of his earlier lied in any other manner; it was always the oboe which carried the melody in his mind, from the moment he composed it for the more practical piano.

The score is interesting. It is really a string piece with two oboes in unison above. The melody is further doubled by all the first violins except for the first desk; while the first desks of second violins, violas and cellos and a solo bass are divided from the rest of their sections. A harp touches in solid chords, mainly *pp*, and it is not until the word 'verklärt' that we hear flutes, clarinets and bassoons for the first time. And at 'ganzen Welt' the *tutti* comprises two horns and a trumpet in addition. (The trumpet plays only five bars and is *tacet* for the last one—an expensive piece of orchestration!) But the effect is masterly, and this is clearly the version of 'Mein Auge' which says everything Strauss wanted to say.

Du bist mein Auge!	You are my eyes!
Du durchdringst mich ganz,	You pierce right through me,
mein ganzes Wesen hast du mir erhellt,	you have illuminated my whole being,
mein ganzes Leben du erfüllt mit Glanz,	filled my whole life with radiance,
mich Strauchelnden auf sichern Pfad gestellt!	and set me on the right path when I strayed!
Mein Auge du!	You are my eyes!
Wie war ich doch so blind an Herz und Sinn,	How blind I was in heart and mind
eh du dich mir gesellt,	before you were by my side,
und wie durchströmt mich jetzt so licht,	and how the glory of this whole world
so lind verklärt der Abglanz	floods through me now,
dieser ganzen Welt!	so bright, so gently radiant!
Du bist mein Auge, du!	You are my eyes—you!

In the piano version the writing is somewhat unclear as to the time-signature of the accompaniment, which seems to be contrary to the vocal line. Although it is written in 4/8, the handfuls of semiquavers fall less distinctly into the pattern of *rest*, 2, 3, 4 than that of 4, 4, 6, 5, 4, 6 and so on. This is why, at first glance, the piano version appears like an exercise in cross-rhythms. As for the pianist himself, what looks formidable is in the end not really so. Seven and eight notes put down at a time turn out to be common chords, for the lied is written almost atonally, with a key-signature of F. The bristling accidentals throughout really mean A major for most of the time. It is a rewarding song nevertheless for both singer and pianist, the first needing a firm *legato* and the second a strong set of fingers.

'Ich schwebe' is one of the frothiest little love-songs Strauss ever wrote. It has to go fairly quickly if the essential joy is not to be dissipated, for a swinging 3/4 time shows the composer's debt to Johann Strauss in a song which smacks of Vienna, though it was composed in Berlin in September 1900.

The accompaniment is very nearly all in sixths, which give an open and clear-sounding texture, not at all earthbound as the singer describes. It comes second in opus 48; the poem is by Henckell.

Ich schwebe wie auf Engelsschwingen, die Erde kaum berührt mein Fuss, in meinen Ohren hör' ich klingen wie der Geliebten Scheidegruss.	I float as if borne on angels' wings, my feet scarcely touch the ground, in my ears I seem to hear my love's parting words.
Das tönt so lieblich, mild und leise, das spricht so zage, zart und rein, leicht lullt die nachgeklung'ne Weise in wonneschweren Traum mich ein.	It sounds so lovely, mild and gentle, speaks so hesitatingly, tenderly and purely; lightly the echoing melody lulls me to sleep, and dream in ecstasy.
Mein schimmernd' Aug', indess mich füllen die süssesten der Melodien, sieht ohne Falten, ohne Hüllen mein' lächelnd' Lieb' vorüberziehn.	My shining eyes, while the sweetest of melodies fill me, see clearly, unimpeded, my smiling love passing by.

The sense of being above the ground is beautifully expressed in the phrase 'kaum berührt mein Fuss' by the placing of a quaver rest before 'berührt', thus suspending the word for a moment. The song is in A major and is marked *Zart bewegt* ('moving tenderly'); there is no orchestral version. It is no song for a beginner, for not only does it lie uncomfortably high for most of the time but it calls for a clear and sparkling delivery that must completely hide the difficulties in placing and breathing; this only a very accomplished singer can provide.

By opus 56 it was evident that Strauss had forsaken the conventional modulations for others more drastic and daring than even Liszt had contemplated, and certainly such as Beethoven would have wondered at. Strauss was equally aware that he sometimes produced 'impossible' modulations (his own word), and in so doing he was proving yet again that he was Germany's leading composer—leading in output, imagination and innovation. But after op. 56 he composed no more lieder for twelve years, and when he did so it was as a changed man, a changed composer and no longer the leader of *avant-garde* German music.

In 1903 Strauss had composed *Taillefer*, his ballad for soloists, chorus and orchestra to words by Uhland. Readings of Uhland had probably also led him to the poem 'Das Tal', the first of two orchestrated songs in op. 51, the other being 'Einsame', by Heine. The Uhland song had been composed before *Taillefer*, and 'Einsame' in 1906, so it is likely that at some time in late 1905 or early 1906 Strauss found three other very strong poems by Heine, one of them being 'Mit deinen blauen Augen'.* Remembering that 1905 was the year of *Salome*, it is characteristic that we find nothing resembling the highly charged emotion of this opera reflected in any of the works near to it—or near to *Elektra*, composed between 1906 and 1908. This set of songs, which falls chronologically between these two most advanced of Strauss's compositions, is thus interesting as the very watershed—in time—of his lieder output. Furthermore, it comes exactly half-way through his life.

'Mit deinen blauen Augen', op. 56, no. 4, is dedicated to Strauss's mother; it is in F major and is marked *Andante*. It is another with the Schubertian style of accompaniment, but of course it is the dramatic Straussian harmonies and modulations which give the bite. Immediately before the last phrase of Heine's poem we have a transition from F major to B major on the syllable 'aller*wärts*', and from the words 'ein Meer' we are in F sharp major until the syllable 'er*giesst*', when Strauss plunges immediately into F again, with a fine result.

Mit deinen blauen Augen siehst du mich lieblich an, da ward mir so träumend zu Sinne, dass ich nicht sprechen kann.	With your blue eyes you look on me sweetly, then my mind becomes so dreamy that I cannot speak.
An deinen blauen Augen gedenk' ich allerwärts: ein Meer von blauen Gedanken ergiesst sich über mein Herz.	Your blue eyes I shall always remember: a sea of azure memories flows over my heart.

The accompaniment, though not difficult, is awkward because of a left-hand cross-over to pick out top notes that complement

* The other two are 'Frühlingsfeier' and 'Die heiligen drei Könige', discussed on pp. 71 and 108 respectively.

the melody. Certain performances and recordings sometimes added an *obbligato* violin part and even allowed an introduction of the melody with violin and piano before the voice came in. There is no warrant for this, nor is there any orchestration of the song from which it could have been taken.

'Mit deinen blauen Augen' was also set by Eduard Lassen and by Delius before Strauss found the poem, but it is Strauss's setting which has survived.

5 *Lusty Songs*

Strauss enjoyed a cigar, a joke and the company of his friends over the skat table in the same way as any German does, though in Strauss's case the jokes were never dubious; the whole proceedings were perfectly decent. From time to time he found poems of a hearty sort, not merely humorous but hefty and bucolic as well, that seem to deserve a category in this book all of their own. I begin with one that might have been placed in the first section but which, in Strauss's musical clothing, becomes a rollicking fairground song for a man to sing. It is called 'Nichts!', to a poem by Hermann von Gilm.

Nennen soll ich, sagt ihr, meine Königin im Liederreich? Toren, die ihr seid, ich kenne sie am wenigsten von euch.	So you want me to tell the name of my queen in the land of song? Fools that you are, I know her less well than any of you.
Fragt mich nach der Augen Farbe, fragt mich nach der Stimme Ton, fragt nach Gang und Tanz und Haltung, ach, und was weiss ich davon!	Ask me what is the colour of her eyes, ask me how her voice sounds ask me how she walks, dances and bears herself, ah, what do I know of all that?
Ist die Sonne nicht die Quelle alles Lebens, alles Lichts? Und was wissen von derselben ich und ihr und alle? Nichts, Nichts.	Is not the sun the source of all life, all light? And what do we know of the sun, I and you and all the rest? Nothing, nothing at all!

It has been said that this is a typically Bavarian song, but I believe that it is the kind which would be enjoyed all over Germany—and Austria, and anywhere else where there is an appreciation of strong, masculine singing.

'Nichts!' is marked *Vivace*; it is in A major and in 3/4 time. There is a further instruction to the singer to 'render freely' and to the accompanist 'with humour'—the only separate stylistic indications which Strauss ever gave to his performers. It is based on the motif:

in the accompaniment, but the vocal line above it is always *legato*, especially in the more romantically tinged centre section where the motif takes a more subordinate part. In bar 35, preparatory to the C sharp major section beginning 'Ist die Sonne', the dotted rhythmic motif gives way to another kind of shape, the Schubert-type accompaniment already noticed in the previous chapter. The triumphant ending, prefaced by the same progression of broken chords as at the beginning of the song, shows how well—how innately well—Strauss was able to give his singer the kind of ending to a song which demands applause. 'Nichts!' is the second song in opus 10, immediately following and greatly contrasted with 'Zueignung'.

'Ich liebe dich' is the second song in opus 37 (following 'Glückes genug') and is to a poem by Detlev von Liliencron. It belies its title, especially in Strauss's setting, and becomes a heroic song, warrior-like and almost Nordic. Strauss has caught up the first verbal phrase 'four prancing steeds', and has set it in common time (one beat for each hoof?) in an unmistakable E flat major. The song is marked 'lively and with fire'. 'Ich liebe dich' is a big song and does not go too well on the piano. The chunky chords and rapid runs are much better, much more appropriate and far more effective in Strauss's orchestrated version, which he produced in August 1943 at Garmisch, at a time of great personal unhappiness.

The song is beautifully composed, and in its enlarged version for double woodwind, 4 horns, 2 trumpets, 3 trombones, timpani and strings it assumes more of a grandiose character. In the piano version the singer starts unaccompanied for one and a half bars, but in the orchestrated edition Strauss has added two bars before the singer's first phrase, sounding on trumpets and two trombones.

An old record with Strauss accompanying Heinrich Schlusnus shows the composer a little discomfited at the extremely taxing piano part which he has written for himself.* However, as in the case of all the few examples we have of Strauss accompanying his own lieder, he plays the notes exactly as written and does not improvise, which is rather a pity.

The poem 'Herr Lenz' is by Emanuel von Bodman, and Strauss has set it as the fifth song in his opus 37 (1896–8). It is in G major (not in the Beethovenish F) and it remains in G major too, which is unusual for Strauss. Only towards the end is there an excursion into E major and then suddenly into A flat on 'Himmels–': a good effect. By then there seems no good reason why the song should not end in A flat, but Strauss only twice ended a song in a different key from the one in which it began.† He boldly cheats with this comic device that is truly in the character of the song and the singer:

Herr Lenz springt heute durch die Stadt	Spring bursts through the town today
in einer blauen Hose.	in blue trousers.
Und wer zwei junge Beine hat,	Anybody with two good legs
springt säftefroh, springt sonnensatt	feels the sap rise and leaps gladly in the sun
und kauft sich bei ihm Lose.	to buy raffle tickets from him.
Dort biegt er um das Giebelhaus,	There he goes, past the gabled house,

* 'Ich liebe dich' was first recorded by Schlusnus and Richard Strauss on an acoustic ten-inch Polydor No. 62364. It has been very well transferred on to an L.P., Rococo 5217.

† 'Wenn . . .' (see note, p. 75) and 'Frühling' (p. 69).

die Taschen voller Gaben,	with his pockets full of presents;
da strecken sich die Hände aus,	everybody holds out his hands
ein jeder möchte einen Strauss—	to get a bouquet
hei! für sein Mädel haben.	hey! to give to his girl.
Ich hole mir auch einen Schatz	I'll find myself a pretty one,
hinweg von Glas und Schüssel.	fetch her away from her chores.
Hut auf! Wir rennen übern Platz:	Hats on! We race across the square:
Herr Lenz, für ihren Busenlatz	'Hey, spring! for her bodice,
ein'n gelben Himmelsschlüssel!	what about a golden cowslip?

The pianist finds himself faced with the need to execute rapid arpeggios in both hands, and thirds in triplets, where Strauss has marked the lower notes small, to indicate that they may be left out. Although the lied is described as 'for a high voice', it is nowadays sung only by dark, masculine voices. It would go well with a soprano for a change.

'Liebeshymnus', op. 32, no. 3, to a poem by Karl Henckell, comes into the present category in the same, surprising way as 'Ich liebe dich'. Neither is a love-song in the same romantic style as those discussed in Chapter 4, and Strauss has found in the words of both of them something which requires a more massive and certainly a more robust treatment. Both, too, are orchestrated. The form which 'Liebeshymnus' takes is not unlike that of 'Wie sollten wir geheim sie halten'* in that the right hand for the first twenty-five bars, out of a total of twenty-nine, plays thick, fat chords of strict quaver value. In the first two bars, the left hand doubles the melody (the singer starts straight in) and plays quavers with the left hand or octaves and broken chords of crotchets. In all there are only eleven dotted notes, so the accompanying effect is very four-square, very rigid. Variation in note-values is given to the singer.

Heil jenem Tag, der dich geboren,	Hail to the day when you were born,
Heil ihm, da ich zuerst dich sah!	hail to the day when I first saw you!
In deiner Augen Glanz verloren	Lost in the glory of your eyes.
steh' ich, ein sel'ger Träumer, da.	I am here, a happy dreamer.

* See p. 30.

Mir scheint der Himmel aufzu- gehn,	The sky seems opened up to me,
den ich von ferne nur geahnt,	which from afar I had only imagined,
und eine Sonne darf ich sehn,	and I can see a sun,
daran die Sehnsucht nur ge- mahnt.	of which only longing reminded me.
Wie schön mein Bild in diesem Blicke!	How wonderful what I see in this apparition!
In diesem Blick mein Glück wie gross!	In this apparition, how great is my fortune!
Und flehend ruf' ich zum Geschicke:	And imploring, I call to destiny:
O weile, weile wandellos!	O stay, stay unchanging!

For once Strauss composed the song in one key (D flat) and transposed it into another (B) when he orchestrated it, and the final result is rather different from the first version. The piano accompaniment dates from 1896, the full one from only a year later, 27 September 1897. Whereas the piano can only hammer out the chunky chords in the left hand which I have already described, this figure is transferred orchestrally to the woodwind. They create entirely the opposite effect, and give the whole song a kind of shimmer. The strings, divided, take the strain of the piece, and below the woodwind, omnipresent horns in quartet and two trumpets (but no other instruments) etch in highlights of this delicate score. I feel there is no other song by Strauss which achieves such different effects in its two forms.

Opus 41, which dates from 1899, contains two songs that might well come in the present chapter. One is 'In der Campagna', which I prefer to place in another group,* but the other definitely belongs here. It is called 'Bruder Liederlich', and is the fourth song in the set. It is in a blunt C major and in 2/4 time; the instruction is to play and sing it in a lively fashion. It is a narrative song, to be sung by a man. The translation will show it to be a merry story; and the poet, Detlev von Liliencron, has enlivened it, thereby making Strauss's task easier, by interspersing from time to time the very singable words 'Halli, Hallo, Halli und Hallo!'

* See p. 88.

Die Feder am Sturmhut in Spiel und Gefahren,
Halli.
Nie lernt' ich im Leben fasten, noch sparen,
Hallo.
Der Dirnen lass' ich die Wege nicht frei,
wo Männer sich raufen, da bin ich dabei
und wo sie saufen, da sauf' ich für drei.
Halli und Hallo.

A feather in my helmet, in play and in peril,
Halli.
I've never learned how to go short of food or money in my life,
Hallo.
I never make way for the wenches,
wherever men are brawling, there you'll find me
and where they are swilling it down I'll swill for three.
Halli and Hallo.

Verdammt, es blieb mir ein Mädchen hängen,
Halli.
Ich kann sie mir nicht aus dem Herzen zwängen,
Hallo.
Ich glaube, sie war erst sechszehn Jahr,
trug rote Bänder im schwarzen Haar
und plauderte wie der lustigste Star.
Halli und Hallo.

Damn it, there was a girl I couldn't get rid of,
Halli.
I can't get her out of my heart.
Hallo.
I think she was only sixteen years old,
she wore red ribbons in her black hair
and chattered away like the merriest of magpies.
Halli and Hallo.

Was hatte das Mädel zwei frische Backen,
Halli.
Krach, konnten die Zähne die Haselnuss knacken,
Hallo.
Sie hat mir das Zimmer mit Blumen geschmückt,
die wir auf heimlichen Wegen gepflückt;
wie hab' ich dafür an's Herz sie gedrückt!
Halli und Hallo, Halli und Hallo.

What rosy cheeks the girl had!
Halli.
Crack, went her teeth on a hazel nut.
Hallo.
She decorated my room with flowers
which we picked on hidden paths;
how I hugged her for that!
Halli and Hallo, Halli and Hallo.

Wie haben süperb die Zeit uns vertrieben,
Halli.
Ich wollt', wir wären zusammen geblieben,
Hallo.
Doch wurde die Sache mir stark ennuyant,
ich sagt' ihr, dass mich die Regierung ernannt,
Kamele zu kaufen in Samarkand,
Halli, Hallo, Halli und Hallo.

We had a marvellous time together,
Halli.
I wish now that we had stayed together,
Hallo.
But the affair began to bore me stiff,
so I told her that the Government had appointed me
to buy camels in Samarkand.
Halli, Hallo, Halli and Hallo.

Und als ich zum Abschied die Hand gab der Kleinen,
Halli.
Da fing sie bitterlich an zu weinen,
Hallo.
Was denk' ich just heute ohn' Unterlass,
dass ich ihr so rauh gab den Reisepass—
Wein her, zum Henker, und da liegt Trumpf Ass!
Halli und Hallo, Halli und Hallo.

And when I gave the little girl my hand at parting,
Halli,
she began to weep bitterly,
Hallo.
Why does it stick in my mind today,
how roughly I sent her on her way—
More wine here. To hell with it! Here's the ace of trumps!
Halli and Hallo, Halli and Hallo.

Considering that Strauss composed this song in 1899, there are some exceedingly daring harmonies and successions of harmonies worth looking at. The first musical phrase is in C major until we get to the first full bar, when a D flat, added to the chord of the seventh instead of a C natural, produces a very unusual and interesting sound. This is repeated a tone higher, four bars later. The following passage illustrates the chordal insecurity which underlines the nature of 'Bruder Liederlich' (which means roughly 'Black Sheep of the Family'), followed by a superficial romantic attachment—a figure which appears from time to time in the song from bar 23:

After the phrases representing the girl weeping at being jilted, the song ends loudly and coarsely with a shout for wine, an oath and a declaration that he has the ace of trumps, followed by the inevitable but now hollow 'Halli und Hallo'. In some respects it is a sad song, especially as certain words indicate that the character is not uneducated: 'süperb', 'ennuyant', 'just', and Samarkand as a place for buying camels. This is a remakably interesting song, not only because of the poem, but also because of the ways in which Strauss saw into the character of the lecher—a kind of Baron Ochs in many ways, but he came eleven years later.

By complete contrast, 'Kling!' is a more refined song altogether; a song of joy of another kind: of gladness and gratitude. It is the third song in the opus 48 set, and was completed in Berlin in September 1900, five days after 'Ich schwebe'.* The poem is by Karl Henckell and the song, in C major and 6/4 time, should be 'very lively and full of energy'. It lies on the top of the treble stave and is therefore most taxing for a soprano; in fact it is deceptively difficult and needs a very agile, almost Zerbinetta-like voice. The accompaniment is mainly made up of arpeggios, and again at the end we see Strauss's favourite trick of seeming to end in a remote key

* See p. 40.

(though not so remote on this occasion) and then switching without modulation, explanation or apology into the key of the signature. The word 'Kling!' occurs twelve times in this short song of only thirty-eight bars, and the chord or arpeggio which begins or ends on the word suggests an orchestral layout in Strauss's mind, a celeste or cymbal clash on each one, certainly a harp *glissando* and swooping string figure. But Strauss never orchestrated 'Kling!', and the pianist has to be most dexterous to keep up the indicated tempo. This is a bright and gay little song, yet its declamatory nature is part of the required effect.

Kling! . . . Meine Seele gibt reinen Ton. Und ich wähnte die Arme von dem wütenden Harme wilder Zeiten zerrissen schon.	Kling! My soul utters a pure sound. And I thought the poor thing had already been destroyed by the terrible afflictions of wild times.
Sing! Sing . . . meine Seele, den Beichtgesang wiedergewonnener Fülle! Hebe vom Herzen die Hülle! Heil dir, geläuterter Innenklang!	Sing! Sing . . . my soul, the confessional-song of regained plenty! Stripping the heart bare, I greet you, purified sound that is within me!
Kling! Kling! Kling! meine Seele, kling dein Leben. kling, kling, quellendes, frisches Gebild! Blühendes hat sich begeben auf dem verdorrten Gefild.	Kling! Kling! Kling! my Soul, ring out your life, kling, kling, spring-like, fresh image! The time of blossoms has begun in the parched fields.
Kling, meine Seele, kling! Kling, meine Seele, kling! Kling! Sing! Kling!	Kling, my soul, kling! Kling, my soul, kling! Kling! Sing! Kling!

The two last songs in this section differ a little from the rest because of their social implications. Ernst Krause has seen Strauss as 'the first lyrical composer of recent times who ventured away from his bourgeois milieu into the realm of social criticism'.* These *Soziallyrik* (socialist lyric) outpourings

* Krause, p. 265.

of the late nineteenth century were barely touched on by Strauss, who was uninterested and untutored in politics to a remarkable degree; yet he seemed to find something in 'Der Arbeitsmann' and then in 'Das Lied des Steinklopfers' which struck a chord of sympathy in him. On the other hand, he may have found the two poems to possess the means whereby he might add further to his musically descriptive powers.

'Der Arbeitsmann', to a poem by Richard Dehmel, finds its place among the complex and intellectual set of songs published in 1898 as opus 39. It is a hard and remorseless setting to equally rough and rugged words that express extreme bitterness, while again the character in the poem who utters them seems, although forced to do the most wretched and demeaning work, to possess some education. The almost military funeral march in F minor which pervades the song has a fearsome—Brahmsian—accompaniment for the pianist, extremely difficult as it is written. Only the last two bars of the song are free of accidentals; and the doleful, pessimistic harmonies, constantly shifting, spell the total unhappiness and hopelessness of the workman. Only mention of walks in the fields on Sundays brings a major key introduction—F major—and the descending thirds with trills to signify the totally free birds. But this is soon turned back into despairing downward thrusts of the piano as it grows in fierceness and intensity. Iron is in the soul of the singer, for time is against him, time—for him—is out of joint.

Wir haben ein Bett, wir haben ein Kind, mein Weib!	We have a bed, we have a child, my wife!
Wir haben auch Arbeit und gar zu zweit,	We also have work—yes, both of us,
und haben die Sonne und Regen und Wind,	and we have the sun and rain and wind
und uns fehlt nur eine Kleinigkeit,	and we need only one little thing more
um so frei zu sein wie die Vögel sind:	to make us as free as the birds are:
nur Zeit, nur Zeit.	only time, only time.
Wenn wir Sonntags durch die Felder geh'n,	When we walk through the fields on Sundays,
mein Kind,	my child,

und über den Ähren weit und breit
das blaue Schwalbenvolk blitzen seh'n,
o dann fehlt uns nicht das bischen Kleid,
um so schön zu sein wie die Vögel sind:
nur Zeit, nur Zeit.
Nur Zeit!

Wir wittern Gewitterwind, wir Volk!
Nur eine kleine Ewigkeit;
uns fehlt ja nichts, mein Weib, mein Kind,
als all' das, was durch uns gedeiht,
um so froh zu sein wie die Vögel sind:
nur Zeit!

and see far and wide above the corn
the blue swallows flash in the sunlight,
oh, then it is not the plumage we lack
to make us as beautiful as the birds are:
only time, only time.
Only time!

We expect the storm wind, we poor people.
Only a short eternity;
and we lack nothing, my wife, my child,
except everything which exists through us,
to make us as happy as the birds are:
only time!

The other song of this kind is 'Das Lied des Steinklopfers', op. 49, no. 4, to a poem by Henckell, which dates from 1900–1. It batters away mercilessly, as the first two bars indicate; and while the singer seems to have some smattering of education—which perhaps makes his plight worse, since he may be presumed to have some sensibility too—he might easily be a drunkard or an ordinary depressed and put-upon working man. The quieter section in the centre of the song tells only half a story about the singer's father, but this soon gives way again to the hammering on the piano which illustrates the stonebreaker's efforts. But no matter how hard he bangs away, the work brings him no satisfaction except—and this is ironical—it is for his country. Yet what good is this to him when he has an empty belly?

Ich bin kein Minister, ich bin kein König,
ich bin kein Priester, ich bin kein Held,
mir ist kein Orden, mir ist kein Titel verliehen worden
und auch kein Geld.

I am no minister, I am no King,
I am no priest, I am no hero,
No decoration, no title has been bestowed on me,
Nor any money either.

Dich will ich kriegen, du harter Brocken,	I will fight you, you hard block of stone,
die Splitter fliegen, der Sand stäubt auf.	splinters fly and the dust flies about.
'Du armer Flegel,' mein Vater brummte,	'You poor lout!' my father growled,
'Nimm' meinen Schlägel,' und starb darauf.	'Take my sledge-hammer,' and then he died.
Heut' hab ich Armer noch nichts gegessen,	Today, miserable fellow, I haven't yet eaten,
der Allerbarmer hat nichts gesandt;	The All-Merciful has sent me nothing;
von goldnem Weine hab ich geträumet	I have been dreaming of golden wine,
und klopfe Steine für's Vaterland.	and I break stones for my country.
Kein Minister, kein König,	No minister, no King,
kein Held! Kein Orden—kein Titel—	no hero! No decoration—no title—
und auch kein Geld.	nor any money.
'Du armer Flegel'—'Nimm meinen Schlägel'—	'You poor lout'—'Take my sledge-hammer'.
noch nichts gegessen—nichts gesandt—	Haven't yet eaten—sent me nothing—
und klopfe Steine für's Vaterland—	and I break stones for my country—
für's Vaterland.	for my country.

Strauss exactly matches the brief quotations from earlier on in the poem with the same line, perhaps rather obvious but still very effective. The song is mainly in quavers in the vocal line, in 4/4, and it appears to be in E minor, though it is most of the time non-tonal, save on the word 'Vaterland' when it jumps into a mock-heroic—and in the context very cynical—E major. But the second time, at the end of the song, the singer is less sure of the rapture in it all, and his voice tails away to remain on B, a note of the scale common to both the major and minor modes, but now definitely minor. The stone-breaking rhythm of the piano slows down too, and it all ends despairingly and definitely in E minor.

6 Sentimental Songs

The songs in this chapter are based on poems which are well and truly a hundred years old; which belong to another century without any doubt at all. Though their images may seem tawdry and overblown, their sentiments ridiculous, their sickliness unpalatable, nevertheless Strauss has made some most wonderful lieder from poems that, while not masterpieces of their time, did at least reflect what the people thought as well as what they seemed to want. One usually finds that such stuff reflects an age of moral restraint, which is partly why it is so difficult to stomach now; but at the time, Strauss found that he had exactly hit the mark with some of these songs, and had not missed it much with the rest. All this made him a great deal of money, but there were times when he preferred not to hear nor to perform those which were sung *ad nauseam.*

Opus 10, to poems by Hermann von Gilm, has as its eighth and last song 'Allerseelen'. This is perhaps Strauss's most purple song, redolent of dark crimson wallpaper, thick, heavy, musty curtains, chenille tablecloths and the peaceful silence of that age which could hang heavily as well. 'Allerseelen' is in E flat major, yet the tone of it all is minor.

Stell' auf den Tisch die duftenden Reseden,	Set on the table the fragrant mignonettes,
die letzten roten Astern trag' herbei,	bring in the last red asters,
und lass uns wieder von der Liebe reden,	and let us talk of love again
wie einst im Mai.	as we once did in May.
Gib mir die Hand, dass ich sie heimlich drücke,	Give me your hand, so that I may secretly press it,
und wenn man's sieht, mir ist es einerlei,	and if anybody sees, it's all one to me,
gib mir nur einen deiner süssen Blicke,	give me just one of your sweet glances
wie einst im Mai.	as you once did in May.

Es blüht und duftet heut' auf jedem Grabe,	Flowers bloom and spread their fragrance today on every grave,
ein Tag im Jahr ist ja den Toten frei,	one day in the year is sacred to the dead,
komm an mein Herz, dass ich dich wieder habe	come to me, let me hold you again,
wie einst im Mai.	As I once did in May.

There are six and a half bars of introduction before the singer enters which give a tranquil feeling, helped by the arpeggios in the left hand of the accompaniment. The piano part does not double the vocal line, in fact it helps it little, and before the first climax on the first 'wie einst im Mai', the accompaniment is in contrary motion to the melody. This climax is overshadowed by the last one, 'komm an mein Herz, dass ich dich wieder habe', in an exultant double forte. All Souls' Day (2 November) is sacred to the dead, and the singer's character is trying to take advantage of the day to revive an old love affair which, it seems, has also died. There is no pity in the song unless it be in the uphill struggle that ends with a question-mark. All the songs in this opus 10 are designed to be sung by a soprano or a tenor, so the message of 'Allerseelen' is not restricted.

Von Gilm's poem was well known in Germany; Eduard Lassen also set it several years later, though his version is never heard today. Strauss never orchestrated 'Allerseelen', but the German composer and opera-conductor Robert Heger did so in 1932; Heger's version was acceptable to Strauss, and indeed he conducted it at his own concerts.

In June 1948, almost exactly a year before he died, Strauss was in Switzerland, where he was composing his *Four Last Songs*. In between two of them he went back some fifty-four years to the first lied in his early opus 27, 'Ruhe, meine Seele', and orchestrated it. He felt that he had not long to live, and the agony of expression in Karl Henckell's poem suited his imagination perfectly. Thus we find a close link between his last group of songs and this other group, composed half a century and two wars before.

'Ruhe, meine Seele' has the most static, even statuesque

accompaniment of all Strauss's lieder. The voice enters in a dreamy, almost expressionless fashion, and in no particular key, floating above the sustained piano chords (which require an enormous left hand to hold them down). There is no harmonic change until the words 'Brandung, wenn sie schwillt!' Here there are six nervous chromatic runs of fourths and fifths in octaves, finishing with a longer one, all filling bars that previously have sustained semibreves. They also manage to give a sudden, impetuous and upward-rushing movement until the word 'Not', which is on a curious discord, the diminished seventh on A, but with a D natural as its root, for one beat only. The last thirteen bars return to the slow, still and reflective opening, ending with an accompaniment that seeks the heights above the treble stave as if moving heavenward. This is in C major, in Strauss's view the key of Heaven.

Nicht ein Lüftchen regt sich leise,	Not a breath of wind softly stirs,
sanft entschlummert ruht der Hain;	gently folded in sleep, the woods are resting;
durch der Blätter dunkle Hülle	through the dark covering of leaves
stiehlt sich lichter Sonnenschein.	steals a ray of bright sunshine.
Ruhe, ruhe, meine Seele,	Rest, rest, my soul,
deine Stürme gingen wild,	your storms raged wildly,
hast getobt und hast gezittert,	you have roared and trembled
wie die Brandung, wenn sie schwillt!	like the breakers as they heave.
Diese Zeiten sind gewaltig,	These are sorely troubled times,
bringen Herz und Hirn in Not—	disturbing both heart and mind;
Ruhe, ruhe, meine Seele,	rest, rest, my soul
und vergiss, was dich bedroht!	and forget what threatens you.

In the orchestral version of the song, the discord on the word 'Not', described above, is strongly emphasized by continuous holding of the D natural for the whole bar in tuba and string basses, not merely for the one beat. It becomes altogether a far more imposing and weighty song in this form, with triple woodwind (but no contrabassoon) and full complement of brass with timpani, celeste and harp. In 1948 'Diese Zeiten sind gewaltig' was an apt, serious and notable phrase, and the whole song had taken on a fresh meaning for Strauss. Although

Strauss could hardly expect performances of the orchestral version of 'Ruhe, meine Seele', considering its instrumental demands, he was merely 'keeping his hand in' with his favourite occupation of scoring.

Although we may very seldom, if ever, have the opportunity to hear the full orchestra in 'Ruhe, meine Seele', there is fortunately a very good performance of it on record* which indicates how transparently the big sound is effected, and the delicacy with which it is worked. There is no denying, though, that Strauss has changed its mood completely by new emphases and an even more gloomy feeling throughout. It cannot be called the same song at all, and this is a startling exception to orchestrated versions of lieder in Strauss's career. He felt here that his own soul was about to be called to rest, and he seems to have sounded the depths of despair and misery on this June day in 1948, between the composition of 'Im Abendrot' and that of 'Frühling'.

The second song in opus 19, which dates from 1885–8, is called 'Breit' über mein Haupt'. It is raven hair that is spread above the singer's head, so that it would seem a more appropriate song for a man to sing, though it is marked 'for high voice'. The song is in G flat major, in common time and marked *Andante maestoso*. In form it is peaceful and undemonstrative, and may even rival the opening of 'Ruhe, meine Seele', for serenity; though some bars of Schubertian flowing accompaniment make a direct contrast with the other song.

The first phrase:

resembles closely one written by Berlioz more than fifty years before in *Lélio*: the swelling string moment in the 'Chant de Bonheur' introduction.

* By Elisabeth Schwarzkopf, with the L.S.O. conducted by George Szell.

It may have been accidental on Strauss's part, but side by side the two are very similar; Strauss may well have heard Berlioz's work performed even if he did not remember the phrase from his own revision of the French composer's treatise on orchestration.

For once Strauss eschews harmonic excursions, and in this lied he seldom strays from the home key of G flat. It is all extraordinarily simple, though unmistakable Strauss, while the words, though sickly, are greatly enhanced by the music. The song has never been orchestrated.

Breit' über mein Haupt dein schwarzes Haar,	Spread above my head your raven hair,
neig' zu mir dein Angesicht,	bend down your face to mine,
da strömt in die Seele so hell und klar	then there will stream into my soul so bright and clear
mir deiner Augen Licht.	the light from your eyes.
Ich will nicht droben der Sonne Pracht,	I do not want to see above me the sun's splendour,
noch der Sterne leuchtenden Kranz,	nor the shining garland of the stars;
ich will nur deiner Locken Nacht	but only the dark night of your tresses
und deiner Blicke Glanz.	and the glory of your eyes.

Following 'Ruhe, meine Seele' in sequence, but very distant from it in every respect, is one of Strauss's first great song successes: 'Cäcilie'. The poem is by Heinrich Hart and it is second in the group of four songs op. 27, every one of which was successful from the moment it was published. Strauss orchestrated 'Cäcilie' three years after the set appeared in its first form, and the result is a clear demonstration of an orchestral piano part. It is very difficult, making huge demands on the player. The key of 'Cäcilie' is E, bright and jubilant, but at the same time excessively lush by Strauss's standards, since the music matches the words so completely.

Wenn du es wüsstest, was träumen heisst
von brennenden Küssen, von Wandern und Ruhen
mit der Geliebten, Aug' in Auge,
und kosend und plaudernd,
wenn du es wüsstest, du neigtest dein Herz!

If you but knew what it means to dream
of burning kisses, of walking and lying
by one's beloved, gazing fondly,
and talking of love,
if you but knew, your heart would soften!

Wenn du es wüsstest, was bangen heisst
in einsamen Nächten, umschauert von Sturm,
da niemand tröstet milden Mundes
die kampfmüde Seele,
wenn du es wüsstest, du kämest zu mir.

If you but knew what it means to be afraid
on lonely nights, while the storm rages around,
when there is none to console
the weary spirit with gentle kisses,
if you but knew, you would come to me!

Wenn du es wüsstest, was leben heisst,
umhaucht von der Gottheit weltschaffendem Atem,
zu schweben empor, lichtgetragen, zu seligen Höh'n,
wenn du es wüsstest, wenn du es wüsstest,
du lebtest mit mir!

If you but knew what it means to live
in the divine, world-creating breath,
to soar lightly up to the heavenly heights,
if you but knew, if you but knew,
you would live with me!

There is much to be said in favour of the piano setting of this song, for the accompaniment falls comfortably under the fingers for once. The left hand has an agile time, but while the chords may at first look clumsy and difficult, they turn out to be fairly well recognizable once one gets into the song. Nevertheless the correct speed (very fast and lively) is only for experts. As for the vocal line, the phrases seem to be chopped up at first, but three times there occurs a phrase of great length (from 'umschauert vom Sturm', to 'kampfmüde Seele',) needing a very exceptional breath control, some resourcefulness so as to know where to breathe, and a good deal of thought behind it all.

The modulations in the centre section come fast and furious, with a most unexpected chord on 'leb*test*' to emphasize the return to the home key:

The orchestrated version of 'Cäcilie' is in the key of E flat, but apart from this semitone difference in key-colour there is one less bar in the orchestral coda than at the end of the piano part.

On arriving at the centre section in the full score, Strauss makes it easier for the harp by giving the player a new key-signature—C flat—the equivalent of the C major passage in the piano version, which remains until the return to E flat.

'Ich trage meine Minne' is the first song in the set opus 32, and dates from 1896. It is also one of the most familiar, one of the most successful in this intensive period of lieder composition. The title is significant, for the obsolete word *Minne* means more than just love, rather Love in its purest, noblest and most selfless sense (as in the *Minnesänger*).

Ich trage meine Minne vor Wonne stumm
im Herzen und im Sinne mit mir herum.
Ja, dass ich dich gefunden, du liebes Kind,
das freut mich alle Tage, die mir beschieden sind.

I bear my love for you with wonder and silence
in my heart and in my soul,
Yes: that I have found you, my darling,
Fills me with joy every day that is granted to me.

Und ob auch die Himmel trübe, kohlschwarz die Nacht, hell leuchtet meiner Liebe gold- sonnige Pracht.	And even if the heaven is overcast and the night is black as coal, Brightly shines my love's gold and sunny splendour.
Und lügt auch die Welt in Sünden, so tut mir's weh, die Arge muss erblinden vor deiner Unschuld, deiner Un- schuld Schnee.	And if the sinful world lies, it saddens me, the wicked will be blinded by your innocence, your snow- white innocence.
Ich trage, usw.	I bear my love, etc.

Henckell's poem has not the repeat of the first stanza, which Strauss brings back to make the lied cyclic, while the repeat is more or less the same in the setting, but with a formal ending.

If one asks why Strauss repeats the first stanza, the answer lies in the form of the poem. The poet's words are reaffirming the first sentiment which he expresses to clinch the matter, in the same, unshakable words and music. It is in Strauss's favourite key of D flat and the first notable point is in the very short (semiquaver) rest before the word 'stumm' (silently), silence letting in silence; although the word which follows is all part of the first musical (and verbal) phrase, so emphasizing the device. The following semiquaver rest before 'herum' matches this, but because of the different sense it has less emphasis. This underlines the way in which Strauss composed: the words always governed his choice of rhythm completely, and accented words had always to have musical accents too, so as to avoid verbal distortion when they were sung. Some of Strauss's critics were fond of declaring that he was given to turning poetry into prose by a too conscious placing of accents: an exaggeration; but the only conscious form of accenting words is the unconscious manner in which they are normally stressed when spoken.

In December 1932, when Strauss was working on the opera *Die schweigsame Frau* with Stefan Zweig, he replied to his librettist in glowing terms of thanks for the second act; and when he got the third and last act, his gratification knew no bounds. Strauss, who rarely showed such immense enthusiasm over anything, appended a quotation from 'Ich trage meine

Minne', the third and fourth lines of the repeated stanza. He felt that he had found the ideal librettist after Hofmannsthal and accordingly told him so, in most personal terms.

Strauss never orchestrated this song, but it is among the four which Robert Heger arranged in 1932–3.

'Sehnsucht', from a poem by Detlev von Liliencron, is the second lied in opus 32, immediately following the one above.

Ich ging den Weg entlang, der einsam lag, den stets allein ich gehe jeden Tag. Die Heide schweigt, das Feld ist menschenleer, der Wind nur webt im Knickbusch vor mir her.	I walked along the lonely road, which I travel, always alone, every day. The heath is silent, the fields are empty of people, only the wind moves in the hedge before me.
Weit liegt vor mir die Strasse ausgedehnt, es hat mein Herz nur dich, nur dich ersehnt. Und kämest du, ein Wunder wär's für mich, ich neigte mich vor dir: ich liebe dich.	The road stretches ahead into the distance, my heart longs only for you, only for you. And if you came it would be a miracle for me, I'd bow down before you: I love you.
Und im Begegnen nur ein einz'ger Blick, des ganzen Lebens wär' es mein Geschick. Und richtest du dein Auge kalt auf mich, ich trotze, Mädchen, dir: ich liebe dich!	At a chance meeting, if you were to cast one look at me, my whole life's destiny would be in that moment. And should you look coldly upon me, I'd defy you, darling, with 'I love you!'
Doch wenn dein schönes Auge grüsst und lacht wie eine Sonne mir in schwere Nacht, ich zöge rasch dein süsses Herz an mich und flüst're leise dir: ich liebe dich.	Yet if your lovely eyes welcome and smile like a sun coming to me through the deep of night, I'd draw your sweet heart close to me and whisper gently to you: 'I love you.'

The thought progression in the poem suggests that the hopeful traveller may never achieve the desired goal anyway, that it is all a daydream.

Strauss bases his setting on the two-bar phrase:

which is how the song starts. The singer comes in where indicated. Thus each bar starts with a flurry, then settles down to the relatively long minim and part-tied crotchet, causing the accompaniment to pause, almost to stop, though the pedal sustains the tied crotchet over into the next bar's semibreve. Then off it goes again: flurry of three-line quavers, minim, down a semitone to the crotchet, and so on (down a tone to the crotchet on the second of each pair in the combined figure).

The vocal line seems to have no root, except for the repeated key-phrase 'ich liebe dich', first in A flat, then in G flat, and finally in A. Although the key-signature says A (or F sharp minor), the important figure quoted above is more E major than anything, despite the F naturals and the F double-sharp; but after that we are more certainly in C sharp, which changes enharmonically to D flat. Before 'Und richtest du' there is a good deal more excitement in the piano-part with the once-quiet end of each bar breaking into thick, broken chords in both hands. And when the singer imagines the loved one's eyes glancing down, there is a positive frenzy of action in the piano part until 'flüst're leise dir', where we are immediately back with the familiar figure for its two-bar duration. Whereupon the final 'ich liebe dich', the crucial fulfilment of the whole poem and song, takes us soaring up in (imaginary) consummation, most tenderly and passionately. The piano resumes its characteristic motif for four bars: when it is based on a firm chord of A major, the right hand executes a delicate, extended cadenza of single notes an octave above the treble stave, leading to a resolved suspension on E.

The lied is notable for the basic two-bar phrase in the piano part—a really noble stroke, this—and of course for the marvellously successful suspension, so unexpected, yet so right. Strauss has far exceeded the brief of early lieder composers in merely matching his music to the words: in this instance he has gone very much further and has made the words bearable.

When 'Freundliche Vision'—op. 48, no. 1, dated 5 October 1900—appeared, it came in for some severe criticism on two counts. First, the pundits suggested that Strauss had composed the piano accompaniment and had then invented a tune to go over the top; and then they were disgusted that this melody is in C sharp major for six bars when the key-signature says D. But what they failed to understand was the very good reason for this.

The dichotomy between the established romantic form embodied in the poem and the *avant-garde* approach which Strauss takes in setting it shows him nearing his greatest years as a composer, when his non-tonality and smashing of most of the musical household gods in the years 1903–8 put the reins of German music in his hands, and conceded him the right to make authoritative anything which came from his pen. In 1900, however, this was not yet perfectly understood, and 'Freundliche Vision' must have seemed an exceedingly daring and impertinent composition.

Nicht im Schlafe hab' ich das geträumt,	I did not dream it when I was asleep
hell am Tage sah ich's schön vor mir:	but in bright daylight I saw the beauty of it before me:
eine Wiese voller Margaritten;	a meadow full of daisies,
tief ein weisses Haus in grünen Büschen;	a white house hidden in green bushes;
Götterbilder leuchten aus dem Laube.	godlike forms gleaming among the leaves.
Und ich geh' mit Einer, die mich lieb hat,	And I walk with one who loves me
ruhigen Gemütes in die Kühle	peacefully into the cool
dieses weissen Hauses,	of this white house,
in den Frieden, der voll Schönheit wartet,	into the peace that, full of beauty, waits

dass wir kommen.	for our arrival.
Und ich geh' mit Einer, die mich lieb hat,	And I walk with one who loves me
in den Frieden voll Schönheit!	into the peace, full of beauty!

The piano part repeats this figure thirty-eight times within the forty bars marked 'restful':

And dreamily taking its way—almost disconnected from the piano, it seems—is the sensuous melody, its rhythm in no way paralleling what else is going on, monotonously, if one listens lower down. The poem expresses a subject which may be imagination, may be reality, it is hard to know which; and in the context of late nineteenth-century German romanticism, the subject was familiar and popular.

Strauss orchestrated 'Freundliche Vision', together with four others round about the same time (from opp. 47, 48 and 49), in the second half of June 1918, during a period of frustration and uncertainty about his future career after the end of the First War. As consolation he turned, as he so often did, to his favourite and most relaxing musical occupation of scoring and finished this song on 1 July 1918. He has given it to 2 flutes, 2 bassoons, 4 horns, 2 trumpets and 2 trombones, with undivided strings. It is in the same key as the piano version, but the direction which Strauss gives to the strings perhaps lets us into his secret reason for starting in the 'wrong' key. He asks them to mute their instruments until the moment when (with scarcely time, even, for a flick) they must remove mutes and go into the key of D from C sharp. This seems to indicate that the beginning of the song really was a dream, and that there is a difference between what is happening and what the poet *thinks* (or wishes to convince himself) is happening.

There is no call for a *tutti* until the word 'Schönheit', while the employment of wind instruments is throughout so discriminating that the texture of the song is no less transparent than in its piano version.

The same poem was also set by Reger a year later than Strauss, but he omitted the first two lines altogether, thus robbing the poem—and his song—of any sense of mystery. He changed one of Bierbaum's original words, the important 'Schönheit' ('beauty') into 'Sehnsucht' ('longing'), which causes some distortion in the meaning. For whatever reason, Reger's song has not lasted.

7 Seasons and Times of Day

A year before he died, Richard Strauss composed four songs with orchestral accompaniment and was at work on a fifth, to poems by Hesse and Eichendorff. In the peace and quiet of Switzerland after the horrors and privations of the Third Reich, Strauss found the energy and inspiration to compose these fragrant songs, to romantic poems of four-line stanzas rhyming ABAB.

The orchestral forces which he uses are nineteenth-century in conception and in application. The song 'Frühling', completed at Pontresina on 18 July 1948, is the lightest scored of the four, needing only harp and horns with the substantial woodwind and strings common to them all.

There are altogether twelve songs with orchestra (including 'Frühling') which Strauss composed straight into full score, and any piano version of these that exists is merely for rehearsal and study. There are also the handful which he orchestrated almost simultaneously with issue of the piano sets, and in these cases both stand equally as authentic. The ample evidence that Strauss thought orchestrally and was not first and foremost a composer for the piano gives to his lieder a fuller, richer and entirely different flavour from those of other composers (notably Schubert) who thought only for voice and piano. Had it not been for Strauss's lifelong experience with the orchestra, as both conductor and composer in the opera house, it is doubtful whether he could have managed to produce such skilful scores as the *Vier letzte Lieder* ('Four Last Songs'). There is a precedent for his having referred to 'orchestrated lieder' himself—in the pair 'Das Tal' and 'Der Einsame', opus 51—otherwise they are *Gesänge mit Orchesterbegleitung* ('songs with orchestral accompaniment'). However, I prefer to think that by calling the four last songs for orchestra *Lieder*, we have reached the fulfilment of Strauss's lieder composition in setting a new type of true lied, always conceived with the big accompanying sound in mind, lifting it above the drawing-room or intimate platform into the world of the symphony orchestra and major concert-hall. And this is where the *Four Last Songs* should most certainly be, and with a singer of great and beautiful voice to sing them.

When Strauss composed these songs, he first set 'Im Abendrot', to Eichendorff's poem, on 6 May 1948, and considered it as a song apart from the group of three songs after poems by Hermann Hesse, although all four were for high voice and orchestra. The Hesse poems are 'Frühling', 'Beim Schlafengehen' and 'September', and bear the finishing dates of 18 July, 4 August and—appropriately—20 September 1948. Strauss is said to have indicated that he wished 'September' to begin the cycle, and it was in the order 'Beim Schlafengehen', 'September', 'Frühling', 'Im Abendrot' that Kirsten Flagstad gave the first performance of the *Vier letzte Lieder* in London with Wilhelm Furtwängler and the Philharmonia Orchestra on 22 May 1950.

Afterwards, Strauss's friend and publisher Dr Ernst Roth published the songs in the order 'Frühling', 'September', 'Beim Schlafengehen', 'Im Abendrot'. This achieves a small song-cycle from spring to September, from going to sleep to the glow of evening and an implied transfiguration. The key-sequence is more appropriate as well: C minor (ending A major); D major; A flat major (really G flat major); E flat major. The only key jump is now seen to be between D and A flat, half-way through, but it is of little consequence.

What probably strikes one most forcibly on hearing 'Frühling' for the first time, and remains in the mind afterwards, is the way in which it moves. The upward-thrusting curve of strings and woodwind, initially in C minor then in A flat minor, like plants straining to burst out of the earth, produces the most remarkable burgeoning effect. But the minor mood soon gives way, like memories of the past winter under ground (and in keeping with the 'twilit caverns') to an expected and comfortable B major for the trees.

In dämmrigen Grüften träumte ich lang von deinen Bäumen und blauen Lüften, von deinem Duft und Vogel- sang.	In twilit caverns I dreamed long of your trees and blue skies, your fragrance and birdsong.

Nun liegst du erschlossen	Now you lie revealed
in Gleiss und Zier	in glistening splendour,
von Licht übergossen	bathed in light
wie ein Wunder vor mir.	like a miracle before me.
Du kennst mich wieder,	You know me once more;
du lockest mich zart,	you beckon me tenderly.
es zittert durch all meine Glieder	My whole body trembles
deine selige Gegenwart!	at your divine presence.

'Frühling' progresses in three great sweeps. First of all comes the initial movement described above; then the voice soars above the orchestra on the word 'Vogelsang', with the *Daphne*-type *melisma* that we associate with nature in all Strauss's compositions which touch on it. This idea is repeated on 'Wunder' in the next stanza, and on 'Gegenwart' at the end, where the singer has one of the longest sung phrases that Strauss wrote. This, the last sweep, finishes a little abruptly perhaps, but in the typical Straussian cadence of unexpected progressions, we end sweetly in A.

'Frühlingsfeier', to words by Heinrich Heine, is Strauss's opus 56, no. 5. It is dedicated to his mother, which is a little surprising, considering the erotic overtones in the song. The poem expresses the ecstasy of the spring Feast of Adonis; its title, curiously enough, can be translated as *Rite of Spring*,* and Heine's poem expresses the cyclic ritual death motif. 'Frühlingsfeier' is a paean of pagan worship from Strauss's beloved Greece.

Das ist des Frühlings traurige Lust!	This is the sad longing of spring-time!
Die blühenden Mädchen, die wilde Schar,	The radiant maidens, the turbulent crowd,
sie stürmen dahin mit flatterndem Haar	dash to the spot with streaming hair
und Jammergeheul und entblösster Brust:	and mournful howls and bared breasts:
'Adonis! Adonis!'	'Adonis! Adonis!'

* Pointed out by Leo Black, on the B.B.C.

Es sinkt die Nacht. Bei Fackelschein	Night falls. By torchlight
sie suchen hin und her im Wald,	they seek hither and thither in the wood,
der angstverwirret widerhallt	which in wild confusion echoes
vom Weinen und Lachen und Schluchzen und Schreien:	with weeping and laughter and sobbing and shrieking:
'Adonis! Adonis!'	'Adonis! Adonis!'
Das wunderschöne Jünglingsbild,	The wondrously beautiful youth
es liegt am Boden blass und tot,	lies on the ground, pale and dead,
das Blut färbt alle Blumen rot,	his blood tints all the flowers red
und Klagelaut die Luft erfüllt:	and the air is filled with the plaintive cry:
'Adonis!' 'Adonis!' usw. (8-mal)	'Adonis! Adonis!' etc. (8 times)

This is the most abandoned of Strauss's lieder so far as the words go, and certainly he has matched these words to perfection in his later orchestral setting. This setting of the song is by far the more interesting; by comparison the piano in the first version seems to be acting as at an early rehearsal as a substitute for the orchestra. The song is scored for triple woodwind; 4 horns, 2 trumpets and 3 trombones; timpani, percussion and strings. There is something in common here with the texture of two of the *Four Last Songs*, although 'Frühlingsfeier' was orchestrated in 1933, and with it Strauss has reached his ultimate formula in transparent colouring of a big song supported by big orchestral forces. After all, he had himself laid down the way to do it in his wonderfully informative preface which he published at the beginning of the full score to his opera *Intermezzo* in 1924, and 'Frühlingsfeier' was the first song which he orchestrated after that date.

It begins in C sharp minor and the soloist has to find her line without any help, save the odd note thrown about from one department to the other among a maelstrom of rushing strings and lower woodwind. The words 'das wunderschöne Jünglingsbild' come as a moment of contemplative peace, where strings and two flutes (mainly in thirds) support the voice for the first time. But at the mention of blood, she is off again. It is a virtuoso song in every respect, and given the right kind of agony in its interpretation, the final six repetitions of 'Adonis!' can wring the heart.

And now to May, with opus 32, no. 4, 'O süsser Mai'. It is a briskly moving, light-as-air little song with a free and fluently moving right hand in the accompaniment, something of a novel layout for Strauss. Harmonically its construction is relatively simple, yet with a wrench at the end so as to get back to the home key of A major which the plea of 'Erbarmen!' does something to alleviate.

O süsser Mai, o habe du Erbarmen,
o süsser Mai, dich fleh' ich glühend an:
an deiner Brust seh' ich die Flur erwarmen
und alles schwillt, was lebt in deinem Bann;
der du so mild und huldvoll ohne Ende,
o lieber Mai, gewähre mir die Spende!

Der düst're Pilger, der in diesen Gau'n
entrann den Eishauch winterlicher Zeit,
erkor ein Mädchen, mild wie du zu schauen,
lenzfrisch gleich dir in keuscher Herrlichkeit.
Dass wir uns lieben und in Lieb umarmen,
Erbarmen, Mai, Holdseligster, Erbarmen!
dass wir uns lieben und in Lieb' umarmen,
Erbarmen,
Erbarmen!

O sweetest May, have pity,
O sweetest May, passionately I implore you:
on your breast I see the field quicken
and everything which lives under your spell increases;
you who are so gentle and full of endless graciousness,
o beloved May, grant me these gifts!

The gloomy pilgrim who, hereabouts,
escaped the icy breath of winter time,
has chosen a maid, gentle as you to gaze on,
fresh as spring, like you, in chaste magnificence
So may we love and embrace one another in love,
Have pity, May, most lovely, have pity!
So may we love and embrace one another in love,
Have pity!
Have pity!

The song is a fairly taxing one for the accompanist, for the right hand scarcely keeps still at all, and when it does it is only for two semiquaver rests in each bar of sixteen marked *Lebhaft* with this pattern:

The singer finds herself high up in the treble stave, though seldom above it, and this area is usually the most searching for the soprano voice. The phrases are long and the vocal line is practically continuous. Instead of a flourish on the end with an upward-moving phrase, Strauss still faithfully follows the natural cadence of the word and brings 'Erbarmen!' downwards.

Carl Busse's poems 'Blauer Sommer', 'Wenn . . .' and 'Weisser Jasmin' are almost a set in themselves, yet Strauss tacked on to them another, quite different song called 'Stiller Gang', which is unique among his lieder composition, if indeed it can be called a lied.* However, we are concerned

* See p. 106.

here with 'Blauer Sommer', the first of the opus 31 set, composed in 1895–6. The Busse songs were dedicated to Strauss's sister, Johanna, on 8 July 1895.

'Blauer Sommer' was composed at the same time as the earlier sections of *Also sprach Zarathustra*, but there is no direct connection to be found, in thought or impression, between the fat, glowing summer song and the long, rambling musical translation of Nietzsche. If there is any connection at all between this set and the 'new age' of Nietzsche, it must surely be in the following song, 'Wenn . . .', which became notorious in its own time.*

'Blauer Sommer' starts with an unusual progression of chords thus:

It modulates so far away from its B major start that Strauss resorts to an action almost unprecedented in his lieder composition, giving a key-change to cancel out all the sharps. The song moves to A flat and then towards sharp keys again, with some uncertainty in the accompaniment, and with use of the diminished seventh, as if provision is being made to leap off in any direction. But the singer gives the lie to all this for she is safely in D; and then the key-signature is changed back for our return to B. The ending is very still and calm, with the reiterated words 'rot von Rosen' being breathed most gently as if it is all a miracle:

* 'Wenn . . .' begins in E flat and ends, purposely and with a deliberate key-signature change, in E; and there is a note to the singer to transpose the ending down a semitone if it is still the nineteenth century!

In a sense, perhaps the kind of a summer day which the song evokes *is* a kind of a miracle.

Ein blauer Sommer glanz- und glutenschwer	An azure summer, glowing with light and warmth,
geht über Wiesen, Felder, Gärten her.	moves across meadows, fields and gardens.
Die Sonnenkrone glüht auf seinen Locken,	The sun's crown glows on summer's curls,
sein warmer Atem läutet Blütenglocken.	its warm breath makes the flowers' bells ring.
Ein goldnes Band umzieht die blaue Stirne,	A golden band encircles the blue brow;
schwer aus den Zweigen fällt die reife Frucht	ripe fruit falls heavily from the boughs,
und Sens' und Sichel blitzt auf Flur und Feld,	and scythe and sickle flash in field and meadow;
und rot von Rosen,	and red with roses,
rot von Rosen ist die ganze Welt.	red with roses is the whole world.
Rot von Rosen.	Red with roses.

And from summer to winter. Strauss composed four songs which have the word *Winter* in their titles, the earliest (1871) being the Jugendlied 'Winterreise',* whose name at once conjures up the Schubert song-cycle. The poem is by Ludwig Uhland, not by Schubert's poet, Wilhelm Müller.

Bei diesem kalten Wehen	In this cold wind
sind alle Strassen leer,	the streets are all empty;
die Wasser stille stehen;	the waters are still

* Once called opus 1.

ich aber schweif' einher,	but yet I roam about.
die Sonne scheint so trübe,	The sun shines so gloomily
muss früh hinuntergehn,	it must early start to rest;
erloschen ist die Liebe	when love is dead
die Lust kann nie bestehn.	pleasure can never exist.
Nun ist der Wald zu Ende,	Here is the end of the wood
am Dorfe mach' ich halt,	and I'll stop in the village
und wärm' mir meine Hände,	to warm my hands
bleibt auch das Herze kalt,	though my heart remains cold.
usw.	etc.

This sad little poem was set by the seven-year-old Strauss in a manner very reminiscent of Schubert. Particularly so is the phrase for 'wärm' mir meine Hände' the first time it occurs. This is almost exactly the same as that in Schubert's 'Der Wanderer' to the words 'ich bin ein Fremdling überall': the similarity of content in the two poems is not to be ignored either, whether conscious or not.

Strauss's 'Winterreise' goes through simple and perfectly conventional modulations from C minor—the key of the song—to G minor, G major and D major; but his move to A flat minor at 'so trübe' is fresh and unexpected. Although the accompaniment often shadows the melody, and its construction is mainly predictable, the whole song is an extraordinary achievement for so young a boy, and its ending is remarkable. Immediately after the last 'kalt' of all, the left hand has two upward triplet runs in an equivocal G minor/C minor mode, below rising tremolo C minor chords in the right. Apart from the idea, a further unexpected event is the inclusion of F sharp in the left hand, a note which has nothing to do with C minor. The setting has obviously been well thought out, and a further point of interest is in the sustained minim for the singer on 'ein*her*' in the tenth bar, when the piano gives it only a crotchet and a rest. A small point, it is true, but what finesse for a seven-year-old!

The next of Strauss's winter songs is probably the most cheerful—'Winternacht', opus 15, no. 2, dated 1884–6. The poem is by von Schack, and Strauss meets him equally in the opening 'with rain and roaring wind':

Mit Regen und Sturmgebrause
sei mir willkommen, Dezembermond,
und führ' mich den Weg zum traulichen Hause,
wo meine geliebte Herrin wohnt.

Nie hab' ich die Blüte des Maien,
den blauenden Himmel, den blitzenden Tau
so fröhlich gegrüsst, wie heute dein Schneien,
dein Nebelgebräu and Wolkengrau;

denn durch das Flokkengetriebe,
schöner, als jeder Lenz gelacht,
leuchtet und blüht der Frühling der Liebe
mir heimlich nun in der Winternacht
leuchtet und blüht, usw.

With rain and roaring wind
I bid you welcome, moon of December;
show me the way to the snug little house
where my beloved lady lives.

Never have I greeted so gaily the blossoming of May,
the blue of heaven, nor the sparkling dew,
as I greet today your snow,
and your foggy brews and your grey skies;

for through the driving flakes,
lovelier than any laughing spring,
shines and blossoms the spring of love
secretly now in the winter night
shines and blossoms, etc.

It will be seen that the rain and roaring wind are not the real content of this poem, for in spite of the storm raging outside the singer and his lady turn it into an indoor spring with their lovemaking. Strauss points this when he comes out of G minor, D minor and B flat minor and into the tranquil G major passage. Though in reminding us what is still going on outside, the song ends with the first motif, with the penultimate chord (C minor with an added 6th) avoiding the conventional G minor close by going into G major instead.

The two halves of this song have several points of contact, namely the phrase 'und führ' mich den Weg':

with 'das Flokkengetriebe':

denn durch das Flok - ken - ge - trie - - be,
Ped. * Ped. * Ped. * Ped. *

while the phrase 'der Frühling der Liebe':

blüht der Früh - ling der Lie - be mir heim - - lich–
Ped. * Ped. * Ped. *

is straight out of *La Prise de Troie* (Chorebus).*

Moreover, the first chord of the song, on the upbeat of a spare bar, is an interesting idea.

The next song, 'Winterweihe', is only marginally a song about winter, but I include it here because it offers an almost direct comparison with the previous 'Winternacht', so far as the poet's thoughts and Strauss's treatment are concerned. Both poems are about the warmth which is derived from love indoors when it is cold outside. 'Winterweihe' is the better of the two; the poem is by Karl Henckell, who provided four out of the five poems, opus 48, of which this is the fourth. Strauss composed the five lieder in September 1900 in Berlin, a respite from his main task of *Feuersnot*.

In diesen Wintertagen,	In these wintry days,
nun sich das Licht verhüllt,	now that the light is dim,
lass uns im Herzen tragen,	let us carry in our hearts
einander traulich sagen,	and declare to one another
was uns mit innerm Licht erfüllt.	what fills us with an inner light.

* See reference to Strauss and Berlioz, p. 60.

Was milde Glut entzündet, soll brennen fort und fort, was Seelen zart verbündet und Geisterbrücken gründet, sei unser leises Losungswort.	That which kindles a gentle flame will burn and go on burning. That which transmits thoughts and gently unites our souls shall be our whispered password.
Das Rad der Zeit mag rollen, wir greifen kaum hinein, dem Schein der Welt verschollen, auf unserm Eiland wollen wir Tag und Nacht der sel'gen Liebe weih'n.	The wheel of time may roll on and we barely take hold of it, forgotten by the world's vain show on our island shall we dedicate each day and night to blissful love.

Something of the lovers' secrecy is brought out in the right hand of the piano accompaniment, where the singers' notes are concealed inside the chords. Another interesting feature of the poem is its five-line stanzas, which, oddly enough, 'Winternacht' also has. The extra line here is helpful to Strauss in the expansion of his modulations.

The first stanza moves gently—the whole atmosphere of the lied is gentleness— from E flat into G major; the second goes forward into B major, for the mystical reference to the union of souls (a remote key); then, with an enharmonic switch, Strauss comes back into E flat for the third stanza, making great capital of the word 'sel'gen'. This is again in G, but we are then steered carefully back into E flat, repeating those chords with the hidden melody, and emphasizing 'Wintertagen', where, despite everything else that is going on, we undoubtedly are.

Strauss orchestrated 'Winterweihe' in June 1918, probably in one day. He uses what is, for him, a small orchestra: 1 oboe, 2 clarinets, 2 bassoons, 3 horns, 10 each of first and second violins, 6 violas, 6 cellos and 4 basses. The numbers of string players are specified, as are their instructions over mutes. The first desks of violas and cellos are to use mutes, while the other four players in each section are not. Likewise the double basses are divided, one desk with mutes and the other without, to give a firmer bass line at the bottom. The orchestral effect is very dark, and only once do the first violins go higher in their stave than B natural—on the words 'gründet, sei unser' in the second stanza. Otherwise they are kept down on the G string, the bassoons often joining them in unison. In consequence, what I have referred to as 'hidden' notes in the piano version are here much more in evidence. The horns, while having no significant solo to play, help to create a gloomy effect.

In 1907 or 1908, Arnold Schoenberg published his setting of this poem under the title 'In diesen Wintertagen', and Walter Gieseking made a solo piano arrangement of Strauss's song.

On the day after he had scored 'Winterweihe', Strauss scored the song which immediately follows it in opus 48, but for a very much larger orchestra. This is 'Winterliebe', also to a poem by Karl Henckell but altogether different in mood from its companion. As a result Strauss makes a very different lied out of it. His instruction to the singer is 'Very fiery' or 'Very passionate'.

This is unmistakably a song about winter. It describes various seasonal subjects, but by the time that Henckell's third stanza has been reached (Strauss almost treats the whole work as a narrative) we are made aware of the familiar, burning love that overcomes all winter's cold. But this time it is more in parentheses, and some of the German words for 'cracking' and 'creaking' add to the aural picture, while the lines of the programme, by not rhyming, add a jaggedness to it all as well.

Der Sonne entgegen in Liebesgluten wand'r ich . . . o Wonne, wer mässe dein Mass!	Towards the sun with passionate ardour I wander . . . O rapture! Who can fathom your being?
Mit Reif bepudert prangen die Wälder, die Berge grüssen das blendende Licht.	With hoar-frost rimed the woods are resplendent, the mountains greet the blinding light.
Vor Eiseskälte knirschen die Schritte, der Hauch des Mundes ballt sich zu Dampf . . .	In the icy cold the footsteps crackle, breath comes from our mouths as steam . . .
Ich trage Feuer in meinem Herzen, mich brennt die Liebe, das schlimme Kind.	I carry fire in my heart, Love, that naughty child, consumes me

Sie schürt die Flamme	It fans the flames
mit hastigen Händen,	with fast-beating hands,
die Kohlen knistern,	the coals crackle,
der Wohlduft quillt . . .	the air trembles. . .
Der Sonne entgegen, usw.	Towards the sun etc.

One should probably approach a lied from its original version. The march-like rhythm of the piano score is not exactly the flavour that Strauss seems to have had in mind when he orchestrated the song. It sounds very martial despite the many triplets which are trying to break it up.

The full score embraces double woodwind with an additional piccolo, 4 horns, 2 trumpets and 3 trombones. There are also timpani, side-drums and cymbal, and strings. It is a big song in this form. It includes, over and above the piano version, one introductory bar, and here the singer no longer enters unaccompanied on the upbeat. The full version is most certainly more grandiose than the piano setting, but I feel that Strauss may here have slightly overplayed his orchestral hand, may have *overset* the song.

*

'Morgenrot' is a seldom-sung lied in opus 46, dating from the turn of the century, a most productive point in Strauss's lieder-writing career. Between opus 40, *Ein Heldenleben*, and opus 50, *Feuersnot*, came lieder, male-voice choruses and the melodrama *Das Schloss am Meer* for voice and piano. But lieder predominated in a concentrated working span of nearly two years solely devoted to the voice.

None of the opus 46 songs has tempted singers during the first quarter of a century since Strauss died, and it is difficult to understand why. The first of the set, 'Ein Obdach gegen Sturm und Wind', was often sung by Pauline Strauss, and it was to her that Strauss dedicated 'Morgenrot' on her birthday in 1900. It contains a great deal of beauty and interest.

to Ernst Kraus, a superb tenor from Berlin and the first Herod in London in 1910.

The song is numbered opus 49, no. 2, and is to a poem by Paul Remer. The accompaniment which Strauss has given the verse jogs along with a rum-titti-tum-titti, false-heroic rhythm that never seems to let up at all, though there are a few bars where the everlasting dotted quavers are left undotted. Since the German word *Fülle* is rich in meanings, I have varied the translation by using several different ones.

Wir schreiten in goldener Fülle durch seliges Sommerland, fest liegen uns're Hände wie in einander gebannt.	We walk in golden abundance through the sweet summer countryside, our hands are clasped as if bound together.
Die grosse Sommersonne hat uns're Herzen erhellt, wir schriten in goldener Fülle bis an das Ende der Welt.	The great summer sun has illuminated our hearts, we walk in golden abundance to the end of the world.
Und bleicht deine sinkende Stirne und lässt meine Seele ihr Haus, wir schreiten in goldener Fülle auch in das Jenseits hinaus.	And if your brow is pale and my soul leaves its body, we stride through a golden glory on into the hereafter.
Wem solch ein Sommer beschieden der lacht der flüchtigen Zeit, wir schreiten in goldener Fülle durch alle Ewigkeit.	To whom such a summer may be given can laugh at the passing of time. we walk in golden fulfillment through all eternity.
Wir schreiten in goldener Fülle durch seliges Sommerland. Wir schreiten in goldener Fülle bis an das Ende der Welt. Wir schreiten in goldener Fülle durch alle Ewigkeit.	We walk in a golden glory through the sweet summer countryside, we walk in a golden glory to the end of the world. We walk in a golden glory through all eternity.

This may have been a satisfactory, heroic song in 1901, but nearly three-quarters of a century later it seems to mean very little at all, either verbally or musically.

Here is an instance when Strauss had no words on which to build a musical edifice—or at least where the words were not strong enough—and I for one find this the only case in his lieder composition when he failed to produce a good song. The modulations are—in Strauss's language—conventional. There is a move out of the key of A flat into C major on 'Welt' at the end of the second stanza; then into A flat minor for the next two lines, and quickly into A flat major until 'Jenseits' (which, rather obviously, has to be different and is) in F sharp minor, F sharp major. After some flirting with E major, we are there for certain on a long and extended 'Ewigkeit' at the end of the third stanza; then comes a sudden switch into A flat major, where we stay, but there is a surprising though brief four bars in A major for the last line but one, before our 'Ewigkeit' which is resolutely in A flat.

'Traum durch die Dämmerung', a justly famous song, belongs to the year 1894 or 1895 and is the first in opus 29, a set of three songs to poems by Julius Bierbaum. We are told that Strauss was at work on the composition of this song soon after his marriage to Pauline de Ahna, when she came into his study at Hildegardstrasse, Munich, where they lived, and announced that she wished to be taken for a walk. When Strauss mildly pointed out that he was composing and preferred not to be interrupted, she said that she would give him twenty minutes and no more. Punctually returning, she found him ready to go out. The lied was finished.

Strauss's setting is a perfect example of his ability to catch the entire mood of a poem and to enclose it in music which always thereafter belongs to it. Max Reger used the same poem shortly after Strauss had done so, but it is Strauss's version which has lasted.

The lazy figure:

which occurs in every bar for practically the whole of the song, not only exemplifies the romantic nature of the poem, but at the same time expresses the settling-down of daytime into dusk and stillness. The disposition of note-values between the left and right hands of the accompaniment makes sure that there is continuous sound, though we are not exactly aware how this is done, merely by hearing it, any more than we are aware of the diminishing degrees of light at dusk.

Weite Wiesen im Dämmergrau; die Sonne verglomm, die Sterne ziehn, nun geh' ich hin zu der schönsten Frau, weit über Wiesen im Dämmergrau, tief in den Busch von Jasmin.	Broad meadows in the grey twilight; the sun has faded away, the stars appear, now I go to the fairest woman far across the meadows in the grey twilight, deep into the thicket of jasmine.
Durch Dämmergrau in der Liebe Land; ich gehe nicht schnell, ich eile nicht; mich zieht ein weiches, samtenes Band durch Dämmergrau in der Liebe Land, in ein blaues, mildes Licht.	Through the grey twilight to the land of love; I do not go quickly, I do not hurry, I am pulled by a soft, velvet ribbon through the grey twilight to the land of love, into a soft, blue light.
Ich gehe nicht schnell, usw.	I do not go quickly, etc.

When the singer changes the direction of the words from the time of day to the reason for going to meet the 'schönsten Frau', Strauss alters the key-signature, a very unusual expediient for him. It is a big change, from F sharp major to B flat, but the modulation is managed easily enough by pivoting enharmonically on D sharp (E flat). Then, when the words return to nature, Strauss goes back into G flat so that after only eight bars in the changed key he cancels the flats and returns to F sharp. Can the interruption by his wife have occurred at the key-change? It is not beyond his sense of humour to have perpetuated the event in this manner.

'Traum durch die Dämmerung' was never orchestrated by

Strauss, but Heger's arrangement of it has always been regarded as the authentic one.

'In der Campagna', opus 41, no. 2, dating from 24 August 1899, is to a poem by John Henry Mackay. Strauss marks his lied to go 'passionately and full of energy'. It is in E flat, in 4/4 time, and has a number of well-defined figures upon which it is built.

Ich grüsse die Sonne, die dort versinkt,	I greet the sinking sun,
ich grüsse des Meeres schweigende Fluten,	I greet the silent flood of the sea,
das durstig, durstig die Gluten trinkt,	that thirstily, thirstily drowns the embers
die lautlos an seinem Herzen verbluten.	which silently bleed to death on its heart.
Ich grüsse die Ebene, wie liegt sie still	I greet the plain, still lies
des Abends geheimnisvoll dämmernde Weite,	the evening's secretive twilight breadth,
durch die ich, der ich nach Hause will,	through which I, who want to go home
nun schneller und immer schneller schreite!	stride ever faster and faster.
Wie ist die Brust von Glück geschwellt,	How my breast is swelled with happiness!
mich umgaukelt die luftige Schaar	I am surrounded by the airy horde of
meiner Lieder, und ich grüsse die Welt,	my songs, and I greet the world,
diese herrliche Welt!	this glorious world!
Ich grüsse sie, morgen seh' ich sie wieder!	I greet it! Tomorrow I shall see it again!

The Campagna is the plain which surrounds Rome. Strauss frequently visited Italy, and became as familiar with it as he was with his own native country. Inspiration for his purest thoughts and finest compositions came from Greece and from Italy. A poem about the Campagna was bound to appeal to him. The musical figure:

may sound martial, but then another persistent figure, four quavers in tempo and then in triplets, changes the shape and feeling of the song before the voice comes in, above an almost exact repetition of the piano introduction. The energetic left hand fills in semiquaver arpeggios which are again an almost constant feature of the lower accompaniment until, becoming chromatic runs rather than arpeggios, they give way to a version of the first figure, moving downwards at first, then taking a prominent part three times in the song. It is a joyful song, glorifying the elements more than the simple words of the poem.

On page 70 there is an account of the order of composition and usual order of performance of Strauss's *Four Last Songs*. Now I shall go into some detail over two more of them—'Frühling' has already been discussed, following the general notes about the songs.

The song 'Beim Schlafengehen' is sung third when the four songs are performed together (as is usual). It was composed at Pontresina and finished on 4 August 1948. The poem is by Hermann Hesse.

Nun der Tag mich müd' gemacht,	Now that I feel the tiredness of the day,
soll mein sehnliches Verlangen	my deep longing shall
freundlich die gestirnte Nacht	welcome the starlit night
wie ein müdes Kind empfangen.	as a weary child does.
Hände lasst von allem Tun,	Hands, cease your toiling,
Stirn vergiss du alles Denken,	head, forget about thinking,
alle meine Sinne nun	for all my senses now
wollen sich in Schlummer senken.	are longing to sink themselves in slumber.
Und die Seele unbewacht,	And the unguarded spirit
will in freien Flügen schweben,	wants to float on free wings,
um im Zauberkreis der Nacht	so that in the magic circle of the night
tief und tausendfach zu leben.	it may live deeply and a thousandfold.

It is scored for triple woodwind, except that there are 2 piccolos and no contrabassoon; 4 horns, 2 trumpets, 3 trombones and tuba, celeste and strings. Each of the *Four Last Songs* is scored differently, and this one is slanted towards the top, with its extra piccolo and a celeste. The celeste is not used elsewhere in these songs, and we shall see why. There is also a solo violin, which is very important.

'Beim Schlafengehen' begins in A flat major and ends in D flat major. The transition comes—and there is a change of signature—at the A flat in 4/8 *andante*. A moving-up from the basses and cellos, a kind of stirring—peaceful, even remote. The voice enters as if it had already been speaking, not a clear start but in continuation of something already begun. There was a similar instance in 'Morgen!'* and, like that lied, 'Beim

* See p. 33.

Schlafengehen' does not begin in the 'right' key. By the fifth bar we are already in G flat. The semiquaver rest before 'die gestirnte Nacht' is a very good effect, and it is also a practical device which allows the singer to snatch a breath after the long preceding phrase. At 'Kind' the key changes to A major as if the simplicity of childhood needs something less sophisticated than G flat; while by 'Hände' (letter B in the score) we are in C sharp minor, and two bars later, on 'Stirn', in D major. Notice the note-values in the bar 'alle meine Sinne' where Strauss preserves the precise accents on the words while breaking up the rhythm so as to keep the two words inside the bar, and 'Sinne' on a downbeat. By the syllable 'Schlum-' we have moved back again to A flat, but then Strauss takes us into G flat and changes the key-signature as well. The voice ends there, and the woodwind and first horn echo the fact.

Overlapping the last note of this, the leader of the orchestra begins an extended solo. It might be interesting to dwell on two aspects of this solo, and to consider the possibility that Strauss, the old man looking back on his life, was doing so in this song as the singer tells of how she reflected on the past day as she was going to sleep. Strauss hints at one of the most important and successful events in his life, *Der Rosenkavalier*, which is given in the volion solo. It starts:

At the beginning of the trio in the last act one finds this:

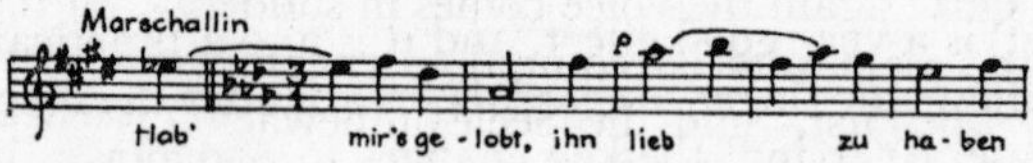

The note-values are different from the example above, but the line is similar.

A little further on, the violin in 'Beim Schlafengehen' takes up a familiar figure (letter D)—very reminiscent of the big duet for Ariadne and Bacchus at the end of *Ariadne auf Naxos*, another subject which may have been in Strauss's thoughts as he was 'going to sleep'.

Again the same figure, although in *Ariadne* the note values are double those in 'Beim Schlafengehen':

Now begins a sequence which is probably the main vocal feature of the whole song (letter E), for it must determine the kind of singer who sings it—and, in fact, sings the other three songs as well. It has the kind of *melisma* which we associate with

Daphne in the opera of that name more than with any other opera or lied. Once again the voice comes in suddenly, on the dominant of the scale, and is required to encompass several huge phrases. The first, 'und die Seele unbewacht' is fairly comfortable. The next, ideally all the way to the end of 'freien' is much harder; then from 'Flügen' to 'Nacht' is scarcely humanly possible and must be broken, but only once. The next phrase, beginning 'tief', is the most problematical of all. It is not possible for most singers to maintain it in one breath, and the break must come, either (and ideally) before 'zu', or, more likely, between '-send-' and '-fach'.

'Beim Schlafengehen' is technically a very difficult song, not only from the point of view of its breathing requirements, which are of a kind that sorts out the women from the girls, but from the interpretative aspect as well. Because of the long phrases with few words, it is more than ever necessary for the singer to project her thoughts and not merely to sing the notes. However clear and fluent and well pitched they may be, the song will not be worth listening to if there is no thought behind the notes.

And as 'Beim Schlafengehen' began with a movement upwards in quavers in the strings, so it ends with the little *Ariadne* triplet phrase moving downwards, sinking, disappearing. Sleep has come, suddenly.

'Im Abendrot' follows, in the revised sequence of the *Four Last Songs*, after 'Beim Schlafengehen', although it is to another man's poem and it was composed first of the four. Strauss dedicated it, with an eye to the pun, to Ernst Roth, and it was completed in Montreux on 6 May 1948, six months after Strauss's return to Switzerland from London. There, Dr Roth and Sir Thomas Beecham had been instrumental in rehabilitating the composer, both musically and politically, in the minds of a somewhat suspicious world—yet a world amazed that Strauss still lived—and had laid foundations for his future successes, which he never lived to see.

The title of this song means literally 'In the evening glow'. Its grand, heavily orchestrated start sets out a plain and simple theme, with the same thought expressed by crotchets as by dotted crotchets; also by interestingly tied and varied values of notes that demand attention. I find the start of this song immensely gripping and moving.

It is in E flat, and starts in common time, though, as we shall see, the lengths of bars will depend upon the requirements of the words in the line.

Wir sind durch Not und Freude gegangen Hand in Hand; vom Wandern ruhn wir [beide] nun überm stillen Land.	Through trouble and joy we have walked hand in hand; we can rest from our wanderings now, above the peaceful country- side.
Rings sich die Täler neigen, es dunkelt schon die Luft, zwei Lerchen nur noch steigen nachträumend in den Duft.	The valleys fall away around us, the sky is already darkening, Only a pair of larks still rise dreamily into the scented air.
Tritt her und lass sie schwirren, bald ist es Schlafenszeit, dass wir uns nicht verirren in dieser Einsamkeit.	Come here, and let them fly For soon it will be time to sleep and we must not lose our way in this solitude.
O weiter, stiller Friede! So tief im Abendrot, Wie sind wir wandermüde— ist dies etwa der Tod?	O broad, contented peace! So deep in the sunset glow, How exhausted we are with our wanderings— can this then be death?

The words of all the *Four Last Songs* indicate how much Strauss was aware of his impending death—almost exactly a year later. It was not so much a death-wish as a normal and perfectly wholesome resignation to the inescapable. He was saying so as he alone knew how.

As soon as the voice enters, Strauss perpetuates the changes of time already indicated in the orchestral introduction. Frequent alteration to the time-signature from common time to 3/2 and back again, and to and fro, is not at all fussy, it is completely calculated. It also helps us to understand the uncertainty and the wandering of which the words tell. This change in measures goes on for most of the song, until one is no longer aware of the mechanics involved.

At letter B a new figure emerges—new that is, to this song, though it has a familiar shape:

It expresses the emergence from difficulties (Strauss's during the war) until now, hand in hand, they (he and Frau Strauss)* pass through the new key of B major to the peaceful land which develops into F sharp minor.

The call of larks takes us back again, for a moment, to the opening scene of *Der Rosenkavalier* (the *Lerchen* and the Lerchenau is something which had not occurred to me before). The rest of the song is predictable in shape and in content after the layout we have had so far, in use of figures seen and heard and in the harmonic progressions, save for two aspects. On the word 'Friede!' we get nine triplet crotchets to the basic structure of 3/2 bars into which we are still coming and going. At letter G ('ist dies etwa der Tod?') Strauss takes seven bars to ask the question, in an air of mystery, awe and hushed suspense, slowing down as if the whole machinery of life and of the song is dying. Then he quotes, very gently as if half heard (though meaning it to be very much heard), the *Verklärung* motif of sixty years before from *Tod und Verklärung*, thus recalling his

* In his refreshing and worldly-wise book *The Business of Music* (Cassell, 1969) Dr Roth describes how, after Strauss's journey by air to London in 1947 and his return to Switzerland, 'on 1 November Frau Pauline could embrace her Richard in Montreux again. With relief and compassion I saw the two old people talk, with tears in their eyes, of the days of their separation'.

own early impressions of a dying man in the tone-poem. Evidently he considered that what he had said then was still valid in 1948. It comes in once like a whisper and then, very slowly, more and more slowly and majestically, the song ends with larks' trills. In fact it is the larks which are still there and have the last word (musically), swooping and rising in the clear air as if to guide the soul upwards and away. Life goes on.

The progression of chords which leads to this ending is very interesting and spreads a feeling not so much of gloom or of the hearty sonority of *Tod und Verklärung* as of peace and optimism.*

'Im Sonnenschein' is to a poem by Rückert and is one of Strauss's later lieder for voice and piano—in this case it is for a bass singer. It belongs to a set of four poems, all by Rückert, dated 1935.

This lied moves quickly. It is a nature song, and while it has gentle and reflective undertones, the singer is able to assert himself strongly.

Noch eine Stunde lasst mich hier verweilen	Just one more hour let me linger here
im Sonnenschein,	in the sunshine,
mit Blumen Lust und Gram des Lebens teilen	the joy and sorrow of life to share with the flowers
im Sonnenschein!	in the sunshine.
Der Frühling kam und schrieb auf Rosenblättern	Spring came and wrote on rose-leaves
ein Traumgedicht vom Paradies,	a dream-poem of paradise,
ich las die goldnen Zeilen	I read the golden lines
im Sonnenschein.	in the sunshine.
Der Sommer kam, das Ird'sche zu verzehren	Summer came to consume the earthbound
mit Himmelsbrand,	with heaven's fire;
ich sah die Ros' erliegen seinen Pfeilen	I saw the rose succumb to its arrows
im Sonnenschein.	in the sunshine.

* The progression is C flat major, A flat minor with an added F natural, B flat major, E flat major, D major, F major, A flat major, D minor, E flat major, C flat major/minor, E flat major.

Es kam der Herbst, das Leben heimzuholen;	Then came autumn, to fetch life home
ich sah ihn nahn, und mit der Ros'	I saw it draw near, and with the rose
in seiner Hand enteilen	in its hand hasten away
im Sonnenschein.	in the sunshine.
Seid mir gegrüsst, ihr Bilder all des Lebens!	Greetings to you, pictures of life!
Die hier ich sah um mich verweilen,	which I saw, lingering around me here,
mir vorübereilen	hurrying past me
im Sonnenschein.	in the sunshine.
Seid mir gegrüsst, ihr Wanderer des Lebens!	You are welcome to me, you wanderers through life!
Die ohne mich und die mit mir gewandert einige Weilen	which without me and with me wandered several times
im Sonnenschein.	in the sunshine.
Zurück ich blick' und seh die Blumentäler	I look back and see the flowery valleys
so leicht durchwallt, und selbst den Berg,	so easily traversed, and also the mountain,
einst schwer erstiegen, steilen	once climbed with difficulty,
im Sonnenschein.	steep in the sunshine,
Ich geh, die süsse Müdigkeit des Lebens	I am going now to rest from the sweet fatigue of life,
nun auszuruhn, die Lust,	to heal the pleasure, and pain of the world,
den Gram der Erde nun auszuheilen	
im Sonnenschein.	in the sunshine.

The song ranges through all the seasons, finishing up with old age, yet it is always about sunshine: the ending of a life, the ending of a day.

Strauss sets the word 'Sonnenschein' in three descending notes of equal value, with either a tone or else a tone and then a semitone between them, except for the last repetition, which is very much more extended.

There is nothing especially remarkable—for Strauss—in the harmonic structure of this song. One is led into strange, remote keys as usual, but it is clearly a tonal song, with a dotted quaver motif, sometimes in the left hand of the accompaniment, sometimes in the right, sometimes inverted, usually in the major mode. It is this, and the invariable shape of the word 'Sonnenschein' when sung, that give the song its character, together with the benevolent feeling which the seventy-one-year-old composer was able to give to such a sentiment.

The autographs of this song and its companions in the set now known as opus 87 indicate that Strauss did not intend to have them published in his lifetime, since they still bore the opus number 81 when discovered after his death, this being the number in fact given to the opera *Friedenstag*, completed in 1936 and first performed in 1938. That the songs were given an opus number at all showed that Strauss considered them to be worth bringing out, and so their posthumous number of 87 merely follows the last numbered work, op. 86, the Divertimento, composed in 1941. A revision of Strauss's opus numbers seems called for.

'Die Nacht' is a song of trembling and yearning, a song tinged with fear that the night, which takes away the familiar shapes of daylight objects, will also steal the beloved. Night and woods are favourite settings for Strauss—for any romantic German, for that matter—and it is not the first time that he has treated verse about them. But this time it is very different.

The song is a gentle *andantino* in 3/4 time—though more properly in 6/8, since the pervading notes in a bar, especially in the right hand of the accompaniment, are quavers. They form a very simple, staccato support for the vocal line (marked *Sotto voce*), painting the picture of night, stepping gently on tiptoe over the ground. The first bar has one note to a beat, the second a chord of two, the third three, the fourth introduces the left hand as well, and gradually the piano forces are built up as if night is becoming more assured with each few, perhaps six, paces that she takes. The skill with which Strauss has employed the two instruments of piano and voice to such remarkable effect is extraordinary. A pretty little poem of sixteen lines is now elevated by sheer genius to become a lied. It is opus 10, no. 3.

Aus dem Walde tritt die Nacht,	Out of the forest steps Night,
aus den Bäumen schleicht sie leise,	out of the trees she softly steals,
schaut sich um in weitem Kreise,	looks around her in a wide arc;
nun gib acht.	now take heed!
Alle Lichter dieser Welt,	All the lights of this world,
alle Blumen, alle Farben	all the flowers, all the colours
löscht sie aus und stiehlt die Garben	she extinguishes and steals the sheaves
weg vom Feld.	from the fields.
Alles nimmt sie, was nur hold,	She takes everything, all beauty,
nimmt das Silber weg des Stroms,	she takes the silver from the stream,
nimmt vom Kupferdach des Doms	and from the copper roof of the cathedral
weg das Gold.	she takes the gold.
Ausgeplündert steht der Strauch,	The bushes are left, stripped naked;
Rücke näher, Seel' an Seele;	come closer, soul to soul.
o die Nacht, mir bangt, sie stehle	I'm so afraid lest night should steal
dich mir auch.	you away from me as well.

Strauss manages to convey the manner in which the all-embracing power of night is stealing so mercilessly over everything: first by a powerful (though gentle) rhythmic beat; and then by the minor seconds (two adjacent black and white notes put down together) which create an effect of merging two objects into one another until they resolve into something else, musically as well as visually.

The key-changes and relationships have been very easy to follow, and still are, when a B flat is introduced on 'näher' (an easy enough move from D major to D minor, which contains B flat); but the powerful change from the dominant seventh in D major to B flat major on the word 'auch' makes the last word of the song the most important, for it means 'as well'. It comes with a heart-rending wrench. The harmony seems to collapse and then to return in an entirely different atmosphere. Even now the new and strange chord is not put down but is to be played as an arpeggio, as if the fingers of night are still stretching out. After four disquieting bars of alternating between D and B flat, we arrive in the 'safe' key of D, and so presumably all is well.

'Die Nacht' is a supreme example of Strauss's art, and he may never have managed quite such a triumph again, even taking into account the superb 'Morgen!'

'Nachtgang', by Otto Julius Bierbaum, is the third song in opus 29, composed in 1894 or 1895. It is a dark song, though not grim; solemn, though not mournful; easy to follow melodically when sung, though almost atonal at sight. The key-signature is A flat major, which is how it begins and ends; but in between we migrate. One fascinating device is a return to A flat major on the word 'rein' for one bar, and then away again—into G major.

The melody of the first line of the song—for the singer comes in at once—is heard twice more: once distorted before the beautifully poised and moving last line; then again after it, resolving and imitating itself in the right context as if in a happy ending. Alternatively it may be saying that the walk is about to continue.

Wir gingen durch die stille, milde Nacht,
dein Arm in meinem, dein Auge in meinem.
Der Mond goss silbernes Licht über dein Angesicht,
wie auf Goldgrund ruhte dein schönes Haupt.
Und du erschienst mir wie eine Heilige,
mild, mild und gross und seelenübervoll,
heilig und rein, wie die liebe Sonne.
Und in die Augen schwoll mir ein warmer Drang
wie Tränenahnung.
Fester fasst' ich dich und küsste,
küsste dich ganz leise.
Meine Seele weinte.

We walked through the still and gentle night,
your arm in mine, your eyes gazing into mine.
The moon poured silver light onto your face,
in a golden frame your head rested.
You appeared like a saint to me,
gentle, gentle and tall and with overflowing soul,
holy and pure, like the beloved sun.
And into my eyes there rose a warm pressure
like a presentiment of tears.
I pressed you closer to me and kissed you,
kissed you so gently.
My soul wept.

The meaning of the situation is not altogether clear. Why, I wonder, did the singer's soul weep at the end? Was it for gladness? If so the music does not tell us. Strauss merely seems to indicate that the walk continues. Bierbaum's blank verse does not notice at first, we are so used to rhyming couplets or alternately rhyming lines in these romantic German poems that we take such a pattern for granted. Here is something else, and perhaps it is designed as an inconclusive feature of the story.

A further aspect of the piano accompaniment that I would like to point out is the word 'Sonne' (the beloved sun). The fairly stately accompaniment breaks out into three groups of three quavers to a bar at this point, suddenly giving movement, a dancelike movement to the song, though the words express a nearness to tears.

'Nachtgang' has never been orchestrated. Max Reger once made a solo piano arrangement of it.

Friedrich Rückert's poem 'Nächtlicher Gang' is surely meant to make the blood curdle.* The huge orchestra which Strauss demands is the main reason why performances of this song and its companion in opus 44 are so extremely rare; they are outside the scope of even the most ambitious concert-promoter.

'Nächtlicher Gang' was composed in November 1899, and Strauss dedicated it to the celebrated operatic baritone Karl Scheidemantel. Its stark, gothic story is like nothing else that Strauss ever chose to set; but this nineteenth-century tale of horror is remarkably effective as a poem, immensely more so inside Strauss's pyrotechnical setting:

Die Fahnen flattern im Mitternachtssturm;	The flags flutter in the midnight wind,
die Schiefern knattern am Kirchenturm:	the tiles rattle on the church tower:
ein Windzug zischt,	a gust of wind whistles,
die Latern' verlischt—	the lantern goes out—
Es muss doch zur Liebsten gehn!	I must still go to my love!

* It is as seriously meant as Mussorgsky's *Night on a Bare Mountain*; but all the same one cannot help but be reminded of Malcolm Arnold's comic (but shattering) overture *Tam O'Shanter*, in spite of the geographical difference and Arnold's broader wit.

Die Totenkapell' mit dem Knochenhaus;	The cemetery chapel and the charnel-house;
der Mond guckt hell zum Fenster heraus;	the moon is reflected brightly in the window;
haussen jeder Tritt	out of doors every step
geht drinnen auch mit.	goes right through me—
Es muss doch zur Liebsten gehn!	I must still go to my love!
Der Judengott'sacker am Berg dort herab;	The Jewish cemetery on the hill down there,
ein weisses Geflacker auf jedem Grab;	a white flickering light on every grave;
ein Uhu ruft dem andern: Schuft—	one owl calls to another: Scoundrel!
Es muss doch zur Liebsten gehn!	I must still go to my love!
Drüben am Bach auf dem Wintereis	Across the stream on the winter ice
ein Geplatz, ein Gekrach, als ging dort, wer weiss;	a splashing, a cracking as goodness knows what goes there;
jetzt wieder ganz still;	then all quiet once more
lass sein, was will—	Come what may—
Es muss doch zur Liebsten gehn!	I must still go to my love!
Am Pachthof vorbei; aus dem Hundehaus fahren	Past the farm; out of the kennels come
kohlschwarz zwei	two coal-black dogs
statt des einen heraus,	instead of one,
gähnen mich an mit glührotem Zahn.	gaping at me with red fangs.
Es muss doch zur Liebsten gehn!	I must still go to my love!
Dort vor dem Fenster, dahinter sie ruht,	In front of the window behind which she lies,
stehn zwei Gespenster und halten die Hut;	stand two ghosts keeping guard;
drin schläft die Braut,	inside sleeps my betrothed
ächzt im Traume laut—	groaning loudly in her dreams—
Es muss doch zur Liebsten gehn.	I must still get to my Love.
Es muss doch zur Liebsten . . .	I must still get . . .

One remembers the mixture of comic and tragic effect which Strauss achieved in three of his tone-poems. In *Till Eulenspiegel* the fierceness of Till's death was tempered by the knowledge that it was a fairy-story. In *Don Juan* there is no humour at all, everything is perfectly serious. *Don Quixote* is rather a pathetic tale. But here, in 'Nächtlicher Gang', it is a question of a man running for his life—to his death, and it is all admirably portrayed.

The song is scored for triple woodwind, with an extra piccolo and an E flat clarinet instead of the bass; 6 horns, 4 trumpets, trombones, tuba, timpani, much percussion, a harp and strings, to total 82 players. The numbers of each string player are specified, with an unusually high proportion at the bottom.

The song is indicated as being in C minor. It begins there, certainly, and it ends there with a slow, eleven-bar coda; but the rest of the work is generally non-tonal, rushing along so quickly that it seems unable, with all the goings-on, to remain in any one key. The score is full and complex, and the printed piano version gives nothing but a very faint idea of what it is all about. This is essentially a song for voice and orchestra.

The start is most eerie. Bassoons and two horns play isolated snaps above a roll on kettledrum and bass drum, with a low C plucked on the harp, two to a bar, which is fast at the speed which Strauss asks for. Then the strings rush in from the bottom upwards, flutes skirl and shriek up and down, the harp gives a *glissando* from bottom to top and the horns perform fast chromatic slides. Throughout all this, both drums have been playing loud rolls, so there is a great noise.

When the singer enters, his line is broken up as if he is out of breath, and the intervals in his part are strangely placed. Nothing is lyrical, nothing as expected. Anything can happen at any moment. The repeated last line of each of the poem's stanzas is fairly consistent as starting in a different

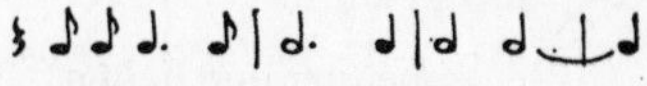

key each time, yet with constant intervals between the notes. But the last time, the singer drops an octave and his last note is a quaver: his death was instantaneous. The pattern of this last, broken-off utterance is

The three works which follow are hybrid songs since they each call for voice, piano and one other instrument. One is an early work; one dates from five years before the turn of the century; and the third comes from opus 56, at the end of Strauss's first period of song-writing. I have singled them out not only because they are, so to speak, rarities, but also because each one is, in its own way, a particularly interesting song.

First comes one of the Jugendlieder, 'Ein Alphorn hör' ich schallen'. It is to a poem by Justinus Kerner and is written for soprano voice, piano and solo horn. It was dedicated to Strauss's father in about 1878, and it is J16 in my list. There is no song of Strauss's which comes nearer in conception (although the poem bears little resemblance) to Schubert's 'Der Hirt auf dem Felsen'; and whereas Schubert needs the clarinet to simulate the shepherd's pipe (the cor anglais would have been far too unwieldy), Strauss gets as near as he can to the sound of the primitive wooden alphorn by using a French horn for the instrument which he had often heard while on holiday with his parents in the mountains. Moreover, the horn was his father's instrument, and Strauss wrote the part with this in mind.

Nearly fifty years later, Strauss took out the work, gave it a dusting and rededicated it to some Viennese friends with the inscription: *This youthful composition which dates from 1876* comes with affectionate good wishes to the dear Mautners from their true friends Richard Strauss and his Pauline. Vienna, 19 March 1926.*

This early song proves beyond question that Strauss was already thinking in terms of a larger sound for lieder than the limited effect of voice and piano. With practice and with discipline, Strauss found that even by thinking of his songs orchestrally, he was still able to confine them to the piano without making them sound insufficient.

* Recent scholarship places the song about two years later than Strauss himself remembered in 1926.

'Ein Alphorn', as a poem, is a typical example of the morbid Kerner, but Strauss in his setting has raised the quality of feeling and has produced a much less melancholy song.

Ein Alphorn hör' ich schallen, das mich von hinnen, von hinnen ruft. Tönt es aus wald' gen Hallen, aus blauer Luft?	I hear an alphorn ringing out calling to me from yonder, from yonder. Does it come from the echoing woods or from the blue sky?
Tönt es von Bergeshöhe, von blumenreichem Tal? Wo ich nur geh' und stehe, hör ich's in süsser Qual.	Does it come from the mountain heights or from the flower'd valley? Wherever I go, wherever I stay I can hear it in sweet suffering.
Bei Spiel und frohem Reigen, einsam mit mir allein, tönt's ohne je zu schweigen, tönt tief ins Herz hinein.	When playing and dancing alone, I hear it always, I hear it deep in my heart.
Noch nie hab' ich gefunden den Ort, woher es schallt, und nimmer wird gesunden dies Herz bis es verhallt.	Never yet have I found the place from whence it comes, and never shall I be myself again at heart, until the sound is gone.

The third stanza is repeated by Strauss immediately as are the two last lines.

The song is in ABA form with a coda; there is an E flat *allegretto* in 6/8 on the outsides and an *andante con moto* for the middle section in E flat minor. 'Ein Alphorn' starts with a firm, though soft, piano chord, followed by a cadenza-like flourish for the horn, very much in the same vein as the start of 'Der Hirt auf dem Felsen' where the clarinet leads off in an extended solo passage with the theme, after a few chords on the piano. But apart from this there is no further point of comparison between the two works.

Here, the voice enters at the end of the tenth bar and the horn is silent, apart from one interjection, until the end of the first stanza of the poem. It is not until the last two lines of the second stanza that we hear the three instruments, voice, horn and piano together; in fact in the centre section, the horn part appears to be little more than an *obbligato* accompaniment.

But it is far more than this. Dramatically it is an integral part of the story, since it is the reason for the tormented singer and her horn-complex. It is the kind of anguished song which was popular in Germany during the last century, but which today sounds rather naïve and sentimental. Whether it is the man blowing the alphorn who is the cause of her distress; whether he is deliberately tormenting her; whether he even knows that she is there—we do not know, and there is nothing in the music to tell us. The fact that the horn part throughout is robustly jolly, in complete contrast to the words, seems to indicate that the horn-player is blissfully unaware that he is occasioning a good deal of pain and grief!

In the outside sections, the piano largely matches the horn's mood with successions of thirds in the right hand; but in the central, minor section, the piano begins in a sinister, ominous manner before sinking into a peaceful Schubert-like accompaniment for the line 'tönt's ohne je zu schweigen', at which point the horn takes up an aggressive, almost perky solo. In the coda, after a general marking of *Lento*, the solo instrument does die away and the song seems to end happily enough.

'Ein Alphorn' possesses no especial harmonic interest, nor any particularly advanced technique, but I include it for its unique combination of the three instruments.

At the end of December 1895, Strauss composed a song for voice, piano and—in an alternative version dated on the same day—solo viola. This is 'Stiller Gang', to a poem by Richard Dehmel, the fourth song in the group of opus 31 and always kept apart from the first three, which are to poems by Carl Busse (of which 'Blauer Sommer'* is the first). All require the normal lieder combination of voice and piano. 'Stiller Gang' is dedicated to Marie, daughter of Strauss's great and artistically influential friend Alexander Ritter, whereas the three other songs are dated July 1895, and dedicated to Strauss's sister Johanna. So 'Stiller Gang' is, for a number of reasons, a kind of appendage to this group, in terms both of temperament and of style. None the less, Strauss must have decided that they belonged together, and they were brought out as opus 31 in 1896.

* See p. 76.

Der Abend graut, Herbstfeuer brennen,	Evening shadows fall and the autumn fires burn;
über den Stoppeln geht der Rauch entzwei.	over the stubble the smoke rises in two columns.
Kaum ist mein Weg noch zu erkennen.	I can scarcely distinguish my way.
Bald kommt die Nacht; ich muss mich trennen.	Soon night will come and I must depart.
Ein Käfer surrt an meinem Ohr vorbei.	A flying beetle whirrs past my ear and then is gone,
Vorbei, vorbei.	is gone, is gone.

This immensely descriptive and strangely sad little song captures the utter stillness and silence of an evening country scene, broken only by the one noise of a beetle, until even that is gone, melted into nature and departed. The German word 'vorbei' has about it the same hopelessness as the English 'too fate', and the viola underlines the sadness of the scene:

In his piano and viola version with voice, Strauss gives the viola, with its particularly rich and melancholy timbre, the line which is shown accented in the solo piano version. One might gather that he lifted this line out of the piano part (although the piano doubles it) and gave it to the viola. But in so doing he makes of 'Stiller Gang' something very similar to Brahms's two songs opus 91 for alto and piano with viola *obbligato*, composed eleven years before. This song lies rather low and can be sung with greater ease by a mezzo-soprano than by a soprano.

A feature in the piano part is the right hand's running accompaniment of often chromatic triplet quavers, sometimes ascending and being taken over by the left hand as it goes down again to the bottom of the bass stave after 'ich muss mich trennen', the point at which the song's climax is reached. This constantly shifting line gives the song an 'atonal' character, though the prevailing key seems to be G minor. At one (poetically) discordant moment it moves into A major with the octave and fifth in the right hand and the C sharp supplied, in passing, by the running bass.

I have already said something about 'Die heiligen drei Könige aus Morgenland' (on page 113 above), the last song in the last set of songs—opus 56—which Strauss composed before the long gap of nearly twelve years between 1906 and 1918. They were followed by the marvellous opus 68 of February 1918, a memorable group which were all orchestrated at a later date.

Although the autograph of the piano version of the 'Drei Könige' is lost, there is no doubt that Strauss composed the orchestral version first and subsequently, in October 1906, rewrote it for piano, at the same time keeping in a trumpet line for six bars in the postlude, though this version is never performed nowadays. The song is scored for 3 flutes, 2 oboes and cor anglais, 2 clarinets, 2 bassoons; 4 horns, 2 trumpets, 3 trombones; timpani and percussion, a celeste and 2 harps; a solo violin and divided strings. It is in this form that I shall first discuss it.

The opening has only the muted lower strings with violas and cellos divided above a held bottom C on the basses, and this continues until the voice enters eighteen bars later. The voice lights up what has until now been a rather dark, foreboding sound, and soon we hear what is to be a feature of the song, frequent arpeggios of the key, C major, in the brass and on the celeste, and in the last phrases by the singer herself.

This song is to a poem by Heine, not to be confused with Hugo Wolf's 'Epiphanie' (Goethe), which starts in the same way.

Die heil'gen drei Kön'ge aus Morgenland,	The three holy kings from the East
sie frugen in jedem Städtchen:	asked in every little town:
'Wo geht der Weg nach Bethlehem,	'Which is the way to Bethlehem,
ihr lieben Buben und Mädchen?'	dear boys and girls?'
Die Jungen und Alten, sie wussten's nicht,	Young and old knew not the answer.
die Kön'ge zogen weiter;	The kings passed on.
sie folgten einem goldenen Stern,	They followed a golden star
der leuchtete lieblich und heiter.	that shone brightly.
Der Stern blieb stehn über Josephs Haus,	The star came to rest over Joseph's house,
da sind sie hineingegangen;	and they went inside.
das Öchslein brüllte, das Kindlein schrie,	The oxen bellowed, the Baby cried,
die heil'gen drei Könige sangen.	the three holy kings sang.

This is the only 'religious' poem which Strauss ever set after the 'Weihnachtslied', and he has created a most moving and penetratingly beautiful song. The grandeur that must have surrounded the Three Kings is verbally matched by the essential simplicity of their destination. From the opening that describes the mystery—and the weariness—of their journey (note the interesting effect in the sixth bar with its triplets); to the bright, golden notes of the celeste; to the uproar when the oxen bellow and the baby cries out—all this is conveyed by the voice; but the final gladness when the kings sing is echoed not by the voice of the soprano but by the whole orchestra, a most touching effect.

The song is in C major, and Strauss's modulations digress into C minor for 'Bethlehem', then to G major/minor. The excitement at 'Stern blieb stehn' is shown in this example taken from the piano version of the song:

At 'sie hineingegangen' I am sometimes uncomfortably reminded of Jokanaan (*Salome* had been performed for the first time the previous year). One finds the same progression of chords in his phrases about Our Lord, which in the context of the opera are not particularly convincing. But here the effect is absolutely right, and one feels that, although Strauss was not at all a religious man, he was greatly moved by this simple poem.

With 'Die heiligen drei Könige', Strauss had achieved a number of things. He had established himself as a profound, active and accomplished lieder composer with a total of 155 songs to his credit. Secondly, and by reason of this, he had learned to write for the human voice in an assured manner so that throughout his next phase of operatic composition he was going to be perfectly at ease and give his singers a number of challenging, though grateful, parts to sing. Thirdly, Strauss had shown in several instances* that he was able to write for voice and orchestra in miniature compositions, an area in which he was to excel.

* In his orchestrations of the lieder 'Cäcilie' (op. 27, no. 2), 'Morgen!' (op. 27, no. 4), 'Liebeshymnus' (op. 32, no. 3), 'Pilgers Morgenlied' (op. 33, no. 4), 'Das Rosenband' (op. 36, no. 1) and 'Meinem Kinde' (op. 37, no. 3), all in 1897.

The years between 1870 and 1906 were by far the richest in his lieder composition, for between 1918 and 1948 Strauss composed only forty-five 'true' lieder for voice and piano (of which seven were later orchestrated) and another seven in his developing style especially for voice and orchestra, which came fully to fruition in the *Four Last Songs*.

So it is with his very last song that I shall end, as I began with his very first, with the 'Weihnachtslied', 78 years and 206 songs before.

Strauss has conjured up in his last finished composition, 'September', the true melancholy of the autumn season. The poem is by his contemporary Hermann Hesse.

Der Garten trauert,	The garden is in mourning.
kühl sinkt in die Blumen der Regen.	Cool falls the rain upon the flowers.
Der Sommer schauert	Summer shudders,
still seinem Ende entgegen.	quietly to its end.
Golden tropft Blatt um Blatt	Leaf after golden leaf drops
nieder vom hohen Akazienbaum.	down from the high acacia tree.
Sommer lächelt erstaunt und matt	Summer smiles, surprised and weary
in den sterbenden Gartentraum.	upon the dying dream of this garden.
Lange noch bei den Rosen	Yet still it lingers by the roses.
bleibt er steh'n, sehnt sich nach Ruh.	longing for rest.
Langsam tut er die [grossen*] müdgewordnen Augen zu.	Then slowly closes its [great*] weary eyes.

The more one hears the *Four Last Songs*, the more one marvels at every aspect of them, the product of a composer whose fresh vitality and inspiration in old age (he was eighty-four) are all the more remarkable when we consider that with *Capriccio* in 1942 he was thought to have had his last say. There is a heavy, throbbing air about *September*, and the feeling is of downward movement throughout, symbolizing the leaves as they fall from the poet's acacia tree. One feels, too, the fall of rain and the shuddering death of summer, sentiments which the poem

* In Hesse's poem, but omitted by Strauss.

and the song express so eloquently. Strauss was ready, like September, to close his own weary eyes on a world that had once, long ago, been like summer to him. Here is complete self-identification.*

'September' is scored for triple woodwind (without contra-bassoon) 4 horns, 2 trombones, harp, and strings which are divided into eleven staves, making a very lush sound indeed. The absence of the lower woodwind and brass instruments helps to lift the texture of orchestral sound and hold it gently poised below the singer. Strauss's deftness of touch here is quite remarkable, and the result which he achieves is a kind of transparent calm.

As in the case of 'Frühling', the soprano voice floats in great vaulted phrases above the orchestra, and a motif:

about a fifth of the way through the song continues to permeate the whole work, reminding us constantly that we are mourning the departure of summer. Nearly every instrument carries this motif, not fugally, not incidentally, but purposefully at one time or another during the song. The first horn takes it up as a valedictory solo at the end. It is a variation of this phrase, shorn of its semi-quavers, with which the work begins and ends, but in a form which does not occur in the voice part:

* *September* is dedicated to Mr and Mrs Seery. Mrs Seery is Maria Jeritza, double creator of Ariadne, and the first Kaiserin in *Die Frau ohne Schatten*. In 1968 she confused the world by announcing to the Press that she had the score of an unpublished song by Richard Strauss which started: 'When at last I close my great weary eyes. . . .'.

The effect of this is one of optimism. Its meaning is plain: that September is not the end, but another beginning, a life hereafter.

One cannot compare these *Four Last Songs*, nor attempt to draw any conclusions as to the various merits of them. Each is different from the others, yet all belong together; however, *September* in particular contains a wealth of subtlety and beauty that repays constant hearing and study. Nothing can ever replace them as a more fitting and glorious epitaph to the last of the great romantic lieder composers.

APPENDIXES

A. Sources of Information on Strauss's Lieder

It is necessary to explain the meanings of other sources of reference which I have quoted against the names of songs in Appendixes, not only for cross-reference purposes for the benefit of readers who have copies of the works concerned, but also to show how scholarship within the short time since Strauss's death has already revealed inconsistencies and former errors.

The most significant reference on the lieder is by Max Steinitzer. It is of prime importance because, as described in Chapter 3, Steinitzer once saw a number of the *Jugendlieder* which have since disappeared, and he alone is able to comment (regrettably briefly) on those that seem no longer to exist; his document is the only means of including them here.

In 1955 a German scholar, Dr E. H. Mueller von Asow, published the first volume of his Thematic Catalogue of all Strauss's works in chronological order, songs included. This and subsequent volumes include everything Strauss wrote: published or unpublished, complete or unfinished, sketched or merely contemplated. There are copious notes about them all.

In 1964 Dr Mueller von Asow died, and his task, which was nearing completion, was taken over by Dr Alfons Ott and Dr Franz Trenner. This led to a change in documentation when fresh material came to light and made it necessary for works to be classified so as to indicate a new position between the numbers allocated already by Asow. Asow had given a number prefixed by AV; now Ott and Trenner introduced oOAV.*

As regards the lieder, I have combined all the Asow, Ott and Trenner information and put the songs into strict chronological order, or as near it as possible where no exact date is stated on

* AV, *Asows Verzeichnis* ('Asow's list'); oOAV, *ohne Opuszahl in Asows Verzeichnis* ('without an opus number in Asow's list').

the score by Strauss. Steinitzer's old order is often useful in such an instance, and so are earlier batches of opus numbers which Strauss once used and then discarded.

Generally speaking, the need for classification applies solely to the *Jugendlieder*; and it is not altogether without possibility that some of the lost songs may yet reappear. There may even be others of which Steinitzer had no knowledge, and of which the Strauss family and Asow had no copies either.

My other principal source is, of course, the four-volume edition of the songs, compiled and published by Boosey & Hawkes in 1964, from the original groups of songs which bore the marks of no less than twelve German and Austrian music publishing houses, as well as their own. Two years later there appeared a supplementary volume, *Nachlese*; this added a little fresh information to the notes in the complete edition, and also gave several songs and sketches not included there.

All other lists and books which I have consulted are subsidiary to the foregoing, but they have none the less been desirable reading to highlight the plain facts.

BIBLIOGRAPHY

ASOW, MUELLER VON. *Richard Strauss Thematisches Verzeichnis.* Doblinger, 1969.

DEL MAR, NORMAN. *Richard Strauss* (vol. 1). Barrie & Rockliff, 1962.

GRASBERGER, FRANZ and HADAMOWSKY, FRANZ. *Richard Strauss Ausstellungs Catalog zum 100 Geburtstag.* Österreichische Nationalbibliothek, 1964.

JEFFERSON, ALAN. *The Operas of Richard Strauss in Great Britain, 1910–63.* Putnam, 1963.

KRAUSE, ERNST. *Richard Strauss, the Man and his Work.* Colletts, 1964.

ROTH, ERNST. *The Business of Music.* Cassell, 1969.

STEINITZER, MAX. *Richard Strauss.* Scuster & Loeffler, 1911.

J1	'Weihnachtslied'	D. F. Schubart	oOAV2	St 1	Dec. 1870
J2	'Einkehr'	L. Uhland	oOAV3	St 2	21 Aug. 1871
J3	'Winterreise'	L. Uhland	oOAV4	St 3	1871
J4	'Des Alpenhirten Abschied'	F. Schiller	AV151	—	?1872
J5	'Der müde Wanderer'	H. v. Fallersleben	oOAV13	St 4	?1873
J6	'Husarenlied'	H. v. Fallersleben	oOAV14	St 5	?1873
J7	'Der Fischer'	Goethe	oOAV33	St 6	1877
J8	'Die Drossel'	L. Uhland	oOAV34	St 11	1877
J9	'Lass ruhen die Toten'	A. v. Chamisso	oOAV35	St 12	1877
J10	'Lust und Qual'	Goethe	oOAV36	St 13	1877
J11	'Spielmann und Zither'	T. Körner	oOAV40	St 7	early Jan. 1878
J12	'Wiegenlied'	H. v. Fallersleben	oOAV41	St 8	early 1878
J13	'Abend- und Morgenrot'	H. v. Fallersleben	oOAV42	St 9	?1878
J14	'Im Walde'	E. Geibel	oOAV43	St 10	early Feb. 1878
J15	'Der Spielmann und sein Kind'	H. v. Fallersleben	oOAV46	St 58	15–28 Feb. 1878
J16	'Ein Alphorn'	J. Kerner	oOAV29	St 69	?1878
J17	'Nebel'	N. v. Lenau	oOAV47	St 14	?1878
J18	'Soldatenlied'	H. v. Fallersleben	oOAV48	St 15	?1878
J19	'Ein Röslein zog ich mir im Garten'	H. v. Fallersleben	oOAV49	St 16	?1878
J20	'Für Musik'	E. Geibel	AV158	St 17	7 Apr. 1879
J21	'Waldesgesang'	E. Geibel	oOAV55	St 19a	9 Apr. 1879
J22	'O schneller mein Ross'	E. Geibel	AV159	St 18	9–10 Apr. 1879
J23	'Die Lilien glühn'	E. Geibel	AV160	St 19	12 Apr. 1879
J24	'Das rote Laub'	E. Geibel	AV161	St 21	May 1879
J25	'Frühlingsanfang'	E. Geibel	AV162	St 22	21–4 May 1879
J26	'Die drei Lieder'	L. Uhland	AV164	St 23	11–18 Dec. 1879
J27	'In Vaters Garten heimlich steht'	H. Heine	oOAV64	St 24	19–24 Dec. 1879
J28	'Der Morgen'	F. v. Sallet	AV165	St 25	9–10 Jan. 1880
J29	'Die erwachte Rose'	F. v. Sallet	oOAV66	St 26	12 Jan. 1880
J30	'Immer leiser wird mein Schlummer'	H. Lingg	AV166	St 27	17 Dec. 1880

J31	'Begegnung'	O. F. Gruppe	oOAV72	—	18 Dec. 1880
J32	'Mutter, o sing mich zur Ruh'	F. v. Hemans	AV167	St 28	29 Dec. 1880
J33	'John Anderson mein Lieb'	R. Burns/Ferdinand Freiligrath	oOAV73	St 29	31 Dec. 1880
J34	'Geheiligte Stätte'	G. Fischer	AV170	St 30	24 Dec. 1881

(Opus 10, *Letzte Blätter*, H. v. Gilm (8)—late Summer, 1882–3)

J35	'Waldesgang'	K. Stieler	AV172	St 31	10 Dec. 1882
J36	'Ballade'	A. Becker	AV173	St 32	? Dec. 1882
J37	'Rote Rosen'	K. Stieler	oOAV76	—	11 Sept. 1883
J38	'Mein Geist ist Trüb'	Lord Byron	AV175	St 33	12 May 1884
J39	'Der Dorn ist Zeichen'	F. von Bodenstedt	AV176	St 34	12 May 1884
J40	'Rosenzeichen'	Anon.	AV180	—	Nov.–Dec. 1886

Opus 15, *Five Songs*—Nov.–Dec. 1886

Some lists of the early songs include, in addition to those given above, an aria from the *Singspiel* 'Lila' (by Goethe) for soprano and orchestra (oOAV 44, and St 56). They also follow it with another setting from the same work for tenor, mixed choir and orchestra (oOAV45, St 57). Since neither belongs with the lieder, I have omitted them. Ott and Trenner also include three fragments and sketches of incomplete songs (oOAV5, 'Waldkonzert', J. N. Vogel; oOAV6, 'Der weisse Hirsch', for three voices and piano; and 'Der bömische Musikant', oOAV7), which I mention in passing for the sake of completeness.

See Appendix 'B' for the mainstream of Strauss lieder, starting with Opus 10, omitting the six last *Jugendlieder* given above (J35–40), but including further lieder without opus numbers in the correct sequence.

C. *The Mature Lieder*

Opus		*Date*
10	Eight Lieder (Gilm)	1882–3
	1 'Zueignung'	
	2 'Nichts'	
	3 'Die Nacht'	
	4 'Georgine'	
	5 'Geduld'	
	6 'Die Verschweigenen'	
	7 'Die Zeitlose'	
	8 'Allerseelen'	
15	Five Lieder	1884–6
	1 'Madrigal' (Michelangelo)	
	2 'Winternacht' (Schack)	
	3 'Lob des Leidens' (Schack)	
	4 'Dem Herzen ähnlich' (Shack)	
	5 'Heimkehr' (Schack)	
17	Six Lieder (Schack)	1885–7
	1 'Seitdem dein Aug' '	
	2 'Ständchen'	
	3 'Das Geheimnis'	
	4 'Von dunklen Schleiern umsponn'	
	5 'Nur Mut'	
	6 'Barcarole'	
19	Six Lieder from *Lotosblätter* (Schack)	1885–8
	1 'Wozu noch, Mädchen'	
	2 'Breit' über mein Haupt'	
	3 'Schön sind, doch kalt, die Himmelssterne'	
	4 'Wie sollten wir geheim sie halten'	
	5 'Hoffen und wieder verzagen'	
	6 'Mein Herz ist stumm'	
21	Five Lieder: *Schlichte Weisen* (Dahn)	1887–8
	1 'All' mein Gedanken'	
	2 'Du meines Herzens Krönelein'	

3 'Ach Lieb', ich muss nun scheiden'
4 'Ach weh mir unglückhaften Mann'
5 'Die Frauen sind oft fromm und still'

22 *Mädchenblumen:* four poems by Dahn 1886–8
1 'Kornblumen'
2 'Mohnblumen'
3 'Epheu'
4 'Wasserrose'

26 Two Lieder (Lenau) 1891
1 'Frühlingsgedränge'
2 'O wärst du mein!'

27 Four Lieder 1894
1 'Ruhe, meine Seele' (Henckell)
2 'Cäcilie' (Hart)
3 'Heimliche Aufforderung' (Mackay)
4 'Morgen!' (Mackay)

29 Three Lieder (Bierbaum) 1894–5
1 'Traum durch die Dämmerung'
2 'Schlagende Herzen'
3 'Nachtgang'

31 Four Lieder
1 'Blauer Sommer' (Busse)
2 'Wenn' (Busse)
3 'Weisser Jasmin' (Busse)
4 'Stiller Gang' (Dehmel) For Voice, Viola & Piano 1895

— 'Wir beiden wollen springen' (Bierbaum) 1896

32 Five Lieder 1896–7
1 'Ich trage meine Minne' (Henckell)
2 'Sehnsucht' (Liliencron)
3 'Liebeshymnus' (Henckell)
4 'O süsser Mai' (Henckell)
5 'Himmelsboten' (*Des Knaben Wunderhorn*)

33 Four Songs for Voice and Orchestra 1896–7
1 'Verführung' (Mackay)
2 'Gesang der Apollopriesterin' (Bodman)

3 'Hymnus' (anon.)
4 'Pilgers Morgenlied' (Goethe)

36 Four Lieder 1897–8
1 'Das Rosenband' (Klopstock)
2 'Für fünfzehn Pfennige' (*Des Knaben Wunderhorn*)
3 'Hat gesagt—bleibt's nicht dabei' (*Des Knaben Wunderhorn*)
4 'Anbetung' (Rückert)

37 Six Lieder 1896–8
1 'Glückes genug' (Liliencron)
2 'Ich liebe dich' (Liliencron)
3 'Meinem Kinde' (Falke)
4 'Mein Auge' (Dehmel)
5 'Herr Lenz' (Bodman)
6 'Hochzeitlich Lied' (Lindner)

39 Five Lieder 1898
1 'Leises Lied' (Dehmel)
2 'Jung Hexenlied' (Bierbaum)
3 'Der Arbeitsmann' (Dehmel)
4 'Befreit' (Dehmel)
5 'Lied an meinen Sohn' (Dehmel)

41 Five Lieder 1899
1 'Wiegenlied' (Dehmel)
2 'In der Campagna' (Mackay)
3 'Am Ufer' (Dehmel)
4 'Bruder Liederlich' (Liliencron)
5 'Leise Lieder' (Morgenstern)

43 Three 'Gesänge' on old German Poets 1899
1 'An Sie' (Klopstock)
2 'Muttertändelei' (Bürger)
3 'Die Ulme zu Hirsau' (Uhland)

44 Two large-scale Songs for low voice & Orchestra 1899
1 'Notturno' (Dehmel)
2 'Nächtlicher Gang' (Rückert)

46 Five Poems by Rückert 1899–1900
1 'Ein Obdach gegen Sturm und Wind'
2 'Gestern war ich Atlas'

3 'Die sieben Siegel'
4 'Morgenrot'
5 'Ich sehe wie in einem Spiegel'

47 Five Lieder (Uhland) 1900
1 'Auf ein Kind'
2 'Des Dichters Abendsgang'
3 'Rückleben'
4 'Einkehr' (second setting—see 1871, J2)
5 'Von den sieben Zechbrüdern'

48 Five Lieder 1900
1 'Freundliche Vision' (Bierbaum)
2 'Ich schwebe' (Henckell)
3 'Kling!' (Henckell)
4 'Winterweihe' (Henckell)
5 'Winterliebe' (Henckell)

49 Eight Lieder 1900–1
1 'Waldseligkeit' (Dehmel)
2 'In goldener Fülle' (Remer)
3 'Wiegenliedchen' (Dehmel)
4 'Lied des Steinklopfers' (Henckell)
5 'Sie wissen's nicht' (Panizza)
6 'Junggesellenschwur' (*Des Knaben Wunderhorn*)
7 'Wer lieben will, muss leiden' (*Elsässische Volkslieder*)
8 'Ach, was Kummer, Qual und Schmerzen' (*Elsässische Volkslieder*)

51 Two Songs for low bass voice and Orchestra
1 'Das Thal' (Uhland) 1902
2 'Der Einsame' (Heine) 1906

56 Six Lieder 1903–6
1 'Gefunden' (Goethe)
2 'Blindenklage' (Henckell)
3 'Im Spätboot' (Meyer)
4 'Mit deinen blauen Augen' (Heine)
5 'Frühlingsfeier' (Heine)
6 'Die heiligen drei Könige' (Heine)

66 *Krämerspiegel* (Kerr) 1918
1–12 (Twelve satirical songs)

67 Six Lieder 1919
Ophelien Lieder (Shakespeare)
1 'Wie erkenn' ich mein Treulieb?'
2 'Guten Morgen, 's ist Sankt Valentinestag'
3 'Sie trugen ihn auf der Bahre bloss'
From the *West-östlicher Divan* (Goethe)
4 'Wer wird von der Welt verlangen'
5 'Hab'ich euch denn je geraten'
6 'Wandrers Gemütsruhe'

68 Six Lieder from Poems by Clemens Brentano 1918–19
1 'An die Nacht'
2 'Ich wollt' ein Sträusslein binden'
3 'Säusle, liebe Myrthe'
4 'Als mir dein Lied erklang'.
5 'Amor'
6 'Lied der Frauen'

69 Five little Lieder 1918–19
1 'Der Stern' (Arnim)
2 'Der Pokal' (Arnim)
3 'Einerlei' (Arnim)
4 Waldesfahrt' (Heine)
5 'Schlechtes Wetter' (Heine)

71 Three Hymns after poems by Hölderlin for high voice and Orchestra 1921
1 'Hymne an die Liebe'
2 'Rückkehr in die Heimat'
3 'Die Liebe'

77 Songs of the Orient (From the Persian and Chinese by Hans Bethge after Hafiz) 1928
1 'Ihre Augen'
2 'Schwung'
3 'Liebesgeschenke'
4 'Die Allmächtige'
5 'Huldigung'

— 'Sinnspruch' (Goethe) from the *West-östlicher Divan* for voice and piano 1919

— 'Durch allen Schall und Klang' (Goethe) from the *West-östlicher Divan* for voice and piano 1925

'87' Four Songs for bass voice and piano

1	'Vom künftigen Alter' (Rückert)	1929
2	'Erschaffen und Beleben' (Goethe) (Hans Adam war ein Erdenkloss)	1922
3	'Und dann nicht mehr' (Rückert)	1929
4	'Im Sonnenschein' (Rückert)	1935

— 'Zugemessne Rhythmen' (Goethe) from the *West-östlicher Divan*, for voice and piano 1935

'88' Three Lieder

1	'Das Bächlein' (anon.)	1933
2	'Blick vom oberen Belvedere' (Weinheber)	1942
3	'St Michael' (Weinheber)	1942

— 'Xenion' (Goethe) 1942

V — *Four Last Songs*, for soprano and Orchestra 1948

1 'Im Abendrot' (Eichendorff)
2 'Frühling' (Hesse)
3 'Beim Schlafengehen' (Hesse)
4 'September' (Hesse)

D. *Poems set by Strauss and other Composers*

Poem	*Poet*	*Opus no.*	*Strauss's pubn. date*	*Other composers*	*Opus no.*	*Pubn. date (others)*
Einkehr	Uhland	J2	*1871*[1]	Kreutzer	34·8	?
O schneller mein Ross	Geibel	J22	*1879*[1]	Delius	—	*1888*[1]
Allerseelen	von Gilm	10, 8	1883	Lassen	85.3	1886
All'mein Gedanken	Dahn	21, 1	1888	Reger	75·9	1904
Du meines Herzens Krönelein	Dahn	21, 2	1888	Reger	76.1	1909
Morgen!	Mackay	27, 4	1894	Reger	66.10	1902
Traum durch die Dämmerung	Bierbaum	29, 1	1895	Reger	35·3	1899
Nachtgang	Bierbaum	29, 3	1895	Reger	51.7	1901
				Berg	—	1904–5[1]
Sehnsucht	Liliencron	32, 2	1896	Pfitzner	10.1	1895[2]
Das Rosenband	Klopstock	36, 1	1898	Schubert	D280	1817[2]
Hat gesagt . . .	*Knaben Wunderhorn*	36, 3	1898	Reger	75·12	1904
Glückes genug	Liliencron	37, 1	1898	Reger	37·3	1899
Meinem Kinde	Falke	37, 3	1898	Reger	43·3	1900
Der Arbeitsmann	Dehmel	39, 3	1898	Pfitzner	30.4	1922
Wiegenlied[3]	Dehmel	41, 1	1899	Pfitzner	11.4	1903
				Reger	43·5	1900
Leise Lieder	Morgenstern	41, 5	1899	Reger	48.2	1900
Freundliche Vision[4]	Bierbaum	48, 1	1901	Reger	66.2	1902
Ich schwebe	Henckell	48, 2	1901	Reger	62.14	1902
Winterweihe[5]	Henckell	48, 4	1901	Schönberg	14.2	1906–7
Waldseligkeit	Dehmel	49, 1	1902	Reger	62.2	1902
Mit deinen blauen Augen	Heine	56, 4	1906	Lassen	—	1878[2]
				Delius	—	*1890–1*[1]

[1] Composition dates in *italics* indicate unpublished songs.

[2] Setting earlier than that by Strauss.

[3] The Pfitzner setting is called *Venus Mater*.

[4] Reger's setting starts later in the poem than Strauss's, at 'Eine Wiese voller Margeritten'.

[5] Schönberg's song is named after the first line of the poem: 'In diesen Wintertagen'.

E. Poets Represented in this Book

BIERBAUM, Otto Julius (1865–1910). His father was a prosperous innkeeper who sent his son to study law and oriental languages with a view to joining the German consular services. His education was interrupted, but he became a successful journalist, then turned to novels and poems. He is no longer fashionable as a writer, but he is important for early promotion of the intellectual cabaret movement in Berlin and elsewhere in Germany, which greatly influenced such men as Frank Wedekind and Berthold Brecht.

Traum durch die Dämmerung, Freundliche Vision, Nachtgang

BODMAN, Emanuel von (born 1874). He was a patriotic, neo-romantic poet, playwright and essayist whose works embrace ten volumes. He died in 1946.

Herr Lenz

BUSSE, Carl (1872–1918). Gained his doctorate at Rostock University in 1898 and went to Berlin to begin a literary career. In 1892 his *Gedichte*, well written, were as well received. He became a lyricist, novelist and literary critic; he was influenced by German romanticism (tempered by realism), and also by von Liliencron (*q.v.*) His novels all deal with the German–Polish borderlands, where he lived.

Blauer Sommer

DAHN, Felix (1834–1912). Professor of law and the author of 'donnish' novels. His great work *Ein Kampf um Rom* (4 vols.) and some small poems are all that remain known today.

Du meines Herzens Krönelein

DEHMEL, Richard (1863–1920). The son of a forester. He studied natural sciences and philosophy before being made editor of a provincial newspaper. Between 1877 and 1895 he was in commerce, but thereafter earned his living from writing. He was one of the founders of the journal *Pan*, whose influence assisted in the formation of the *Jugendstil* school of the arts and literature. His autobiography of reminiscences in the First World War was a testimony to his awareness of the social revolt in Europe; and this is also borne out in some of his poems. But it is by his large output of love-poems that he will be remembered.

Mein Auge, Der Arbeitsmann, Stiller Gang

EICHENDORFF, Joseph Karl Benedikt von (1788–1857). He was brought up in Silesia but studied at the universities of Halle and Heidelberg. In the latter place he met many of the leaders of the German Romantic movement, and began to write poetry from his most formative years there. He fought under both the Prussians and the Austrians in the Wars of Liberation (1810–15), and after the defeat of Napoleon he joined the Prussian Civil Service. Much of his writing describes the dichotomy in his own life: that of the artist longing for freedom and the paid soldier or government official spending his years in an office.
Im Abendrot

GILM ZU ROSENEGG, Hermann von (1812–64). Aristocratic Austrian poet who lived in the Tyrol. He attracted political disfavour by his passionate anti-jesuitical verse, in his striving for political awakening. His lyrics and love-poems reveal a sensitive ear, eye and mind.
Zueignung, *Nichts*, *Allerseelen*, *Die Nacht*

HART, Julius (1859–1930) inseparable brother of Heinrich (1855–1906). They had a joint career as critics, dramatists and poets. They entered the literary life of Berlin intending to reform German literature, and became leaders in its early phrases of naturalistic development. In later years they mellowed and took an active part in religious and socialistic movements. Julius was the author of many fine lyric poems, tragedies, short stories and an outstanding anthology of Spanish poetry.
Cäcilie

HEINE, Heinrich (1797–1856). Of Jewish birth, but later forsook his faith for social reasons, after studying law at Bonn and moving to Berlin. He left Germany after the 1830 revolution, and lived in Paris, where he wrote poems and magnificent prose for the rest of his life. Lieder-composers from Schubert to Strauss have found inspiration in his verse. The last years found him a complete invalid.
Mit deinen blauen Augen, *Frühlingsfeier*, *Die Heiligen drei Könige*

HENCKELL, Karl (1864–1929). A violent socialist and the leader of a revolt in German literature which sought to instil into poetry a new kind of spirit, without robbing it of its traditional form (*see* MACKAY). He emigrated to Switzerland in 1894 because he disapproved strongly of Bismarck and the Prussians, and became a publisher there. His poetry spans the world between the most delicate love lyrics and the bitterest socialist verse.
Ich schwebe, *Liebeshymnus*, *Kling! Lied des Steinklopfers*, *Ruhe meine Seele*, *Ich trage meine Minne*, *O süsser Mai*, *Winterweihe*, *Winterliebe*

HESSE, Hermann (1877–1962). Was placed in a theological seminary by his father, but escaped to earn a living as a bookseller. His short stories and novels, which are both analytical and psychological, deal with the problems afflicting man in the twentieth century. He was awarded the Nobel Prize for Literature in 1946.
Frühling, September, Beim Schlafengehen

KERNER, Justinus (1786–1862). He came into contact at Tübingen University (where he was studying medicine) with Ludwig Uhland (*q.v.*) and other Swabian poets, who kindled in him a love for German literature which never left him. He qualified as a general practitioner, but his poor eyesight obliged him to abandon medicine as a career. He specialized in the occult sciences and recorded his experiences of them. His knowledge of the folk-song coloured his poems which are often tinged with morbidity.
Ein Alphorn hör' ich schallen

KLOPSTOCK, Friedrich Gottlieb (1724–1803). He was a fervently patriotic German poet and contemporary of William Blake, who was very much aware of him. His great religious epic *The Messiah* was inspired by Milton's *Paradise Lost*, and some of his poetry shows great subtlety and tenderness.
Das Rosenband

LILIENCRON, Detlev von (1844–1909). His father was an impecunious baron forced to earn a living as a customs officer, and his mother was the daughter of an American general. Liliencron was a dedicated soldier who served first in the line and then on the staff in both the Austro-Prussian and the Franco-Prussian wars. He was forced to resign his commission on account of debts, and in order to forget both the ignominy and the loss of his chosen mode of life he spent some time in the U.S.A. between 1875 and 1877, as a painter, horse-trader, teacher of piano and of languages, and beer-hall pianist. On his return to Germany he joined the civil service. In spite of his appearance (that of a typical Prussian officer) Liliencron was an extremely sensitive man, very musical and one of the first people in Germany to discover the talents of Hugo Wolf. He exercised great influence on Bierbaum and Busse (*qq.v.*) and on Falke, and his collected poems run to four volumes. Recognition came late to him.
Glückes genug, Ich liebe dich, Bruder liederlich, Sehnsucht

MACKAY, John Henry (1864–1933). He started life in Greenock, Scotland, but was brought up in Germany by a German mother and a Scottish father. He became prominent in Henckell's (*q.v.*) literary

revolt on account of his three novels, one of which was called *Die Anarchisten.* He was a tough individual and a born rebel. He wrote a biography of the individualist philosopher Max Stirner, yet none of his poems show this apparently predominant side of his character.
Morgen!, In der Campagna

REMER, Paul (1867–1943). A minor playwright and poet, and one of the editors of the magazine *Woche* between 1895 and 1902.
In goldener Fülle

RÜCKERT, Johann Michael Friedrich (1788–1866). He took after his father in the study of classical languages and the law. In 1818 he met, in Vienna, the remakable oreintalist Hammer-Purgstall, who influenced him profoundly. From then on he studied and wrote oriental poetry and became Professor of Oriental Studies at Erlangen and Berlin. His poems are seldom simple to understand. He is probably best known as the poet of the *Kindertotenlieder*, written as the result of his own two children's deaths in an epidemic. The poems which Strauss chose to set are all powerful and evocative but do not touch on the oriental.
Morgenrot, Im Sonnenschein, Nächtlicher Gang

SCHACK, Adolf Friedrich von (1815–94). A wealthy aristocrat who was at the same time a diplomat, linguist, traveller and art-collector. He was born in Mecklenburg but made his home in Munich from 1855. The Naturalists admired some of his poems (*see* HENCKELL), but it is his admirable translations from the Persian poets which are among his outstanding contributions to literature.
Ständchen, Wozu noch, Mädchen, Schön sind, doch kalt, Wie sollten wir geheim sie halten, Breit' über mein Haupt, Winternacht

SCHUBART, Christian Friedrich Daniel (1739–91). He was court organist in Stuttgart to Duke Karl Eugen of Württemberg when he chose to utter some outspoken criticism on public affairs: this cost him ten years in jail. His powers and talents as a musician and poet were greater than his tact, and while in prison (1777–87) he wrote a great deal of poetry (among which was *Die Forelle*, immortalized by Franz Schubert), all of which was published before his release. When this happened he was at once appointed director of music at court, while as some sort of a recreation he edited a dubious journal called *Vaterlandschronik*.
Weihnachtslied (original title: *Der Hirten Lied am Kripplein*)

UHLAND, Ludwig (1787–1862). Became a friend of KERNER (*q.v.*). They founded the nucleus of the Swabian poets, based on the impulse of the Heidelberg romantics. He was in Paris in 1810–11, studying medieval manuscripts, and this assisted him to reach the height of his powers. His most creative period was between 1804 and 1817. He became interested in politics while he was professor at Tübingen University from 1824–33. His poetry is inspired by the true tradition of the Volkslied, and there is a great historic sense in his work, although it tends to be impersonal.

Winterreise

Index